BOOK of MEMORIES

BOOK of MEMORIES

Winter Park Presbyterian Church

*60th Anniversary
1953—2013*

iUniverse LLC
Bloomington

Book of Memories
Winter Park Presbyterian Church

iUniverse books may be ordered through booksellers, *Amazon.com,* or by contacting

iUniverse LLC
1663 Liberty Drive
Bloomington, IN 47403
www.iuniverse.com
1-800-Authors (1-800-288-4677)

For all other inquiries and correspondence:
Winter Park Presbyterian Church
400 South Lakemont
Winter Park, FL 32792
407-647-1467
winppc.org
lindal@winppc.org

ISBN: 978-1-4917-1137-8 (sc)
ISBN: 978-1-4917-1138-5 (e)

Photographs from church archives
and by Frank Jamison and others

Cover Design: Matt Straub
Cover Photography: Frank Jamison and church archives

Printed in the United States of America
iUniverse rev. date: 10/28/2013

CONTENTS

APPENDICES

Foreword

Time and tide wait for no man," so the saying goes, meaning that no one is so powerful that they can stop the march of time. What we can do if we choose to live meaningfully is to use the time we have been given to do more than gratify ourselves. We can contribute to the commonwealth as well as to the dignity and well-being of the individual. For that we have been given specific gifts by God to employ in the ongoing story of redemption.

Most of those who read these words are a part of a faith community called Winter Park Presbyterian. Since its inception in the early 1950s this community has sought to respond to God's call to be an outpost of the Kingdom, at the corner of Dundee and Lakemont. They have struggled, triumphed, celebrated, served, given, worshiped, and shared the journey.

A phrase I have used from time to time is "Without our memories we are orphans." The point of a book of memories would be, on one hand, to remind us that we belong – to each other and to God. Simply idealizing the past must not be allowed, but we must realize that we are part of a great ongoing parade of Saints. We are writing the next chapter and can draw inspiration as well as hope for a challenging and sometimes foreboding future. Take heart. There is a "great cloud of witnesses" that has gone before us and now is urging us onward. We march forward, joined arm in arm with a great company of faithful yet very human folks.

Look at the pictures in this book. Let them stir your memories. Recall all of the stories that, taken together, make WPPC the great church it is. These are just ordinary people. At times discouraged, at times elated, at times anxious, at times creative, at times courageous in their faith; but at all times God's people.

Gratefully yours
Dr. C

Dr. Larry Cuthill was Senior Pastor at Winter Park Presbyterian Church from 1993 to 2012.

Preface

Besides being a celebration of our age, our 60th anniversary is a natural opportunity for looking back and taking stock of our history, including its beginnings, the array of events leading to the present, and the parade of people who participated in the process – including those who led. It's a time to reflect, to reminisce, to learn, and to celebrate our blessings with joy.

In late 2012 the Session formed an *ad hoc* History Committee; its first assignment was to create a history book as part of the church's 60th Anniversary celebration in 2013. Our last comprehensive history book was authored by the late Eva M. Bacon, and covered WPPC's first twenty-five years: 1953 – 1978. In the 1990s WPPC historians Delia Delgado, Mildred Baggett, and Pat Williamson embarked on an updated history book to include the first fifty years (1953 – 2003) in a decade-by-decade approach, with the first twenty-five years to be based largely on Eva Bacon's work. That work was not completed, but their notes and documentation are preserved in the church's historical archives.

A significant problem encountered by the History Committee was that, with some exceptions, the storage of accumulated historical artifacts over the years had largely been done on an *ad hoc* basis, with no documented procedures provided to define what should be saved, nor where and how they should be stored. Nor was any equipment provided for this specific purpose other than the storage and file cabinets, bookcases, closets, and boxes that happened to be available at the time. It is to the credit of our Librarian, Myrna Erwin, and other WPPC history supporters that the artifacts have been well preserved and storage of them has largely been confined to the Library and Media Center and Room 315, which was designated a "history room" some years ago, but which is also used for other purposes.

An effort was undertaken and completed in 2012 to inventory the artifacts we have, including their locations. The inventory is contained in a large Word document. All artifacts listed there, along with their outer containers, were physically labeled to reference back to the Word document. We found that many items of no historical value are stored along with the good, many like items are stored separately, and the storage methods and equipment are not conducive to efficient access. We have thousands of photographs without dates or labels of any kind, rendering them less valuable by the day. Digital storage and access are almost nonexistent. There is no permanent office of Historian. Without serious attention, these important assets are at risk.

Given the state of archive storage, the committee concluded that researching and preparing a comprehensive, sixty-year history book in time for the

2013 anniversary celebration was not achievable. Instead, we determined that a *Book of Memories*, with stories contributed by current or former members and friends of the church as they felt inspired, was achievable and would provide an anecdotal view of our history that everyone would enjoy. The response from church members has been wonderful! And we appreciate the unflagging support of our Interim Pastor, Dr. Tim Rogers-Martin. The project has been a work of love and inspiration for the committee.

Thanks to my committee members for carrying on during my surgery and recovery. I am especially grateful to Max Reed, our editor, who was already busy, for taking over as project lead for months in the middle of the project.

Richard Small, Chair, History Committee

Committee Members

Max Reed, Editor	*Barbara Edwards*	*John Gehrig*
Matt Straub, Photo Archivist	*Myrna Erwin*	*Terry Irwin*
Corinne Dodd		*Ginny Seel*

In this poor quality but important photo from September 18, 1955, the first WPPC groundbreaking event takes place for Fellowship Hall and the CE-Preschool Buildings. Taking the first scoop is J. Roy Dickie, Chairman of the Building Committee. Looking on, from left to right, are the Rev. Oswald Delgado, Senior Pastor, Dr. C. Fremont Dale, Acting Moderator and F. E. L. Whitesell, Chairman of the Planning Committee.

BUILDINGS AND GROUNDS

WPPC and the Railroad

by Terry Irwin

Looking at WPPC today, it is almost impossible to tell that a railroad once ran along the southern edge of our church property. What has been smoothed over on the eastern end and is now marked by a ditch on the western end of the property was, even thirty years ago, a recognizable path that had been occupied by railroad tracks. Those tracks are an interesting part of Winter Park history.

WPPC 1959
Lakemont Ave
Dinky RR line
Future parking lot
Future fire station
Fellowship Hall
Future Sanctuary
Dundy Ave

It all started with the Dinky Line, which ran between downtown Orlando and what we now know as the Dinky Dock on the Rollins campus. Built in 1886 and officially known as the Orlando-Winter Park Railroad, it was very popular with students attending Rollins College but living in Orlando. The nickname came from the size of the equipment and even the rails – "They were just dinky."

From the station at what is now Dinky Dock, the rails continued east and south along Lake Virginia, then turned east along the southern shore of Lake Mizell. From there it continued east along the southern edge of the church property to what is now Cady Way Trail. It initially went as far east as Lake Charm in Oviedo and this section was known as the Winter Park-Oviedo Railroad.

Records indicate that the dividing point between the Orlando-Winter Park Railroad and the Winter Park-Oviedo Railroad was Lakemont Station. I have not yet found any records showing the exact location of such a station, but its name suggests that it would have been located very near our western parking lot.

The lines were eventually absorbed into larger railroads, and as the time of the train passed, the rail lines were converted to other purposes: bike trails, walking paths, and in our case, a church.

The Land on Which the Church Stands

by Terry Irwin

In 1925, a group of investors bought 360 acres located southeast of what is now the corner of Lakemont and Aloma. Their intent was to build a country club with an eighteen-hole golf course and then sell home sites bordering the golf course. Aloma Country Club opened in 1925 and in the same year, the Winter Park Country Club closed down. The golf course was completed and formally opened on December 14, 1929. Sales of the home sites did not go as well as expected, however, and by 1936 the Aloma Country Club was shut down.

Because it had made a big investment in the Aloma Country Club, the City of Winter Park bought up much of the land from the failed country club. Several attempts were made to develop the land again, but most remained in the City's possession. In the early 1950s Winter Park Hospital bought several acres and the hospital was built.

In 1953, the Presbytery bought the sixteenth fairway of the old Aloma Country Club golf course for development of a Presbyterian Church in Winter Park. It was approximately three acres in size and cost $5,000.

Our church's initial members met at the Woman's Club of Winter Park and organized the new church. Construction of a physical plant for the church began with building the manse (located on the tee of the old fairway) in September 1953. The first pastor, Reverend Glenn Otto Lantz, and his wife moved into the new manse on January 7, 1954.

The next phase of construction planned after the completion of the manse was an education building and a fellowship hall. This was the education complex that is on the east side of the church, between the fellowship hall and the manse. Ground was broken for this phase on September 18, 1955 and construction was completed in June of 1956. The church now had a place to worship.

In July of 1956, our tie to the old railroad lines came back into focus. A successful cooperative negotiation was completed with Seaboard Airline Railroad to clarify the boundaries of our property.

Construction began in July1958 on the Sanctuary, offices, Chapel, and the west wing of the education building – that is, the classrooms immediately adjacent to the office complex, not the separate two-story building. The first use of the Sanctuary for worship was on July 5, 1959 and its formal dedication took place October 25, 1959.

In January 1965, construction began on the separate two-story Christian Education building. It was designed by the noted architect, James Gamble Rogers II. This building was completed and placed into use in October 1965.

There have been modifications to our buildings over the years, but what we see today was largely complete by 1965.

Mary's Window

by Corinne Jordan Dodd

One of my very earliest memories is that of the church and the lovely central stained-glass window in Peachtree Presbyterian in Atlanta. It shows a larger-than-life Christ ascending into Heaven. I think that inspired my love of stained glass windows, and I find myself taking photographs in cathedrals and churches when I travel. I choose the most meaningful to me, and try to catch the light and the full beauty of the colors and design.

Of them all though, my favorite is the one I see in our Sanctuary every Sunday from "my pew." The Annunciation Window is one I have gazed at hundreds of times since I joined the church with my parents in 1960. Our family always sat in the same spot on the far right, next to that beautiful window.

I moved back to Atlanta after marrying, but returned to Winter Park in 1983 with my own young family, and we found ourselves in that same pew, where I could look at the angel bringing Mary the news of her special baby.

While all our windows in the Sanctuary and the chapel are beautiful, the Annunciation Window will always be special to me. I have loved it and looked at it along with three generations (now that I have granddaughters, four generations) of my family – right there in the same familiar place.

Chapel Stained Glass Windows

by Ginny Seel

The stained glass windows in the chapel were designed and produced by the J. Piercy Studio of Orlando, Florida. They were placed in the chapel during the summer of 1992.

The chapel was built in 1958, as part of the original 1955 plan for the church. It was named the Delgado Chapel in January of 1991, in memory of Dr. Oswald Delgado.

At that time, a committee was formed to consider replacing the original windows. It was decided that the funding for new windows would be solicited through memorial gifts and donations from members and friends of the congregation. In addition, profits from Dr.

Delgado's book *Come Before Winter* were donated for this purpose.

The theme "Our Father's World" and the scripture from the creation story in the book of Genesis were suggested by Dr. Delgado.

The window that depicts "light" (Genesis 1:3) is the first window on the east side of the chapel. Also on that side are windows depicting "land" (Genesis 1: 9-10) and "flora" (Genesis 1:11-12). The west-side windows depict "water" (Genesis 1: 6-8) and "fauna" (Genesis 1:7-8).

It was hoped that these windows would further honor and glorify God, encourage prayer and meditation, and inspire children and those of all ages to experience the wonders of His beautiful world.

Remaking the Church Library

by Myrna Erwin

Having lived in the Palma Ceia part of Tampa for some twenty-five years, my minister-husband was asked to come to Winter Park Presbyterian on a temporary assignment after his retirement. As soon as I could complete my job as a substitute teacher in a public school in Tampa, I joined him to be in Winter Park for six months. It was nice that our son had begun his work in this area and we could see him often.

Our stay at Winter Park extended much longer than we had planned. We would work at Winter Park in the winter and enjoy three months of the summer at our cottage in the mountains. In 1989 things changed. My husband became ill and had to resign. We continued living as we had lived in the past until 1994, when he died of a heart attack in Winter Park.

We had become a part of the Winter Park community and the Winter Park Presbyterian Church. Our son had chosen Winter Park as his home. It seemed natural for me to continue to live in Winter Park. I moved to a condominium near the center of my previous activities and began to build a new life.

I was healthy and had a degree in Christian Education. I asked the DCE if there was something that I could do in the church. She immediately said yes. She would like for me to remake the Church Library. I had had no experience in library work, but I believed that this was where God needed me to serve.

The DCE was a children's educational specialist, and it was in the children's section of the Library that we started. The main Library room, as it was then arranged, was too small for the children's section. The children's books were in a room adjoining the main Library. The plan was to have all of the books in the same room, and some rearrangement was definitely needed. The books for children were moved into the main Library, new children's tables and chairs in bright color were purchased, and new book shelves were built by one of the talented volunteer men of the church.

The rest of the Library needed to be refurbished to be compatible with these new additions. To provide space, shelves were placed along the windowed wall and were built as high as could be accessible.

With the help of another church member, the Resource person in the Presbytery Resource Center, all the books were indexed by age. Books that were not by classic writers or theologians and were published before 1960 were placed in boxes to be given to organizations that could use or sell them.

New methods began to change in the way books were processed. The public library gave us a reference to a company that produced a library computer program. The church processed books by typewriter at that time. The library computer program was purchased, and the volunteer librarians took computer classes and recruited a retired person with computer skills. The new program was learned, a new computer and computer supplies were purchased, and the process of redoing all the books in the Library began. It was a joint effort with many volunteers helping that made this project a success.

New books needed to be purchased to update new information and methods. Research was done to find books with the newest and best information for the church leaders and members to use as they grew in their faith and service. Purchasing new books was expensive. The Tower Circle established the Eliza Callan Library Gift Fund to honor one of the Tower residents, who was a teacher by profession. The purpose of this fund was to purchase new library books.

Church members gave money to this Gift Fund, and thus made it possible to purchase costly books such as commentaries, Bibles, and other expensive resource book. A gift of several thousand dollars was given as a memorial for the purchase of children's books. Another large gift was given that established a video section. Another gift was given to establish a section of Christian Fiction and Biographies of Christian statesmen.

Today, there are more than 5,000 books in the library. The Library is now accessible through the church website. A computer is located in the main Library for visitors to find books by subject, title, or author.

What is in the future? No one knows, but it is believed that books will always be necessary for enlightenment and knowledge. This church has believed from its beginning that God speaks to His people through the written word, and this church has been able to provide this resource for His people to learn about Him. God continues to allow two of the original volunteers to serve, even though it is hard to find places for candles on their birthday cakes.

Sunlight and Stained Glass

by Phyllis Woods

I love the beauty of the stained glass windows in our church, and I love the feeling of the prayers of the people during our prayer time.

There are times I have been in the Sanctuary alone, with sunlight streaming through the stained glass windows, and I'm so aware that the ardent prayers of the people have been received by our gracious Lord.

CHRISTIAN EDUCATION

Christian Education: Its Beginning

from the Archives

Helen Drylie (1958) and Imogene Bennett (1960) were the early Christian Educators that established the framework for the Education work at Winter Park Presbyterian Church. Helen began the organizational establishment for the Educational program for the first two years and Imogene expanded and perfected it in her nine years in the program. The Sunday School started with fifty-three people in 1953 and increased to seven hundred when the new building was finished and twenty-six classrooms were available in October 1959.

Weekday School began in 1959 with Mrs. Virginia Bailey and Mrs. Mary Miller. The Boy Scout Troop #64 was organized through the Men of the Church with Mr. Vernon Derr as the First Scoutmaster. The first Vacation Bible School was held in June 1956. The first Christian Education Committee began their work in February 1957 to care for the increased membership and large Sunday School classes, and to establish criteria for Bible Study and personal Christian growth throughout the membership.

The Christian Educator, Imogene Bennett, gave special attention to the church Library and introduced the Dewey Decimal System as a way to identify our library books in early 1960.

The Living Nativity was inaugurated in December 1960, under the leadership of Imogene Bennett. It became a community institution and is still presented as a vital mission of the church. One year when it was decided not to have it, the community objected, and told the church that it must continue. It was a community tradition.

In 1961 forty-four young people were received by the Session and recognized as members of the church. College Students Sunday in 1961 had thirty-nine college students recognized during the morning worship service. In 1962 the Vacation Bible School attendance was recorded at 319 students and 128 teachers and helpers.

Our Years at WPPC

by Bob and Betty Case

During college we went mainly to the Disciples of Christ Church and Sunday School. I went also to the Methodist Church and Sunday School, but rarely to the Presbyterian Church. I grew up in the Methodist Church, Betty Gale in the Disciples of Christ.

We graduated and I was commissioned in the U.S. Navy one day and we were married the next, in a Methodist chapel. During our moves in the Navy, we were pastored by Methodist (mainly), Baptists, Lutherans, and Disciples of Christ (several of these were Navy chapels). We sponsored youth groups at two places, and I taught Sunday School to middle school, high school, and adult groups at several churches.

We came to Orlando in 1973. It was a thriving, small, beautiful city with I-4 running through the center. Its main purpose was to get you to Disney World quickly (it was not a parking lot then).

We first attended a Methodist Church, but had difficulties there. In1975 we came to Winter Park Presbyterian. At that time, it was probably at its Golden Age. Oswald Delgado was the Senior Pastor and Bruce Cumming was a retired Korean missionary and calling minister. Glenn Bass was a retired Buffalo Bills football star and adult mentor (greatest hugging pastor I have ever known), and Ken Shick was a handsome young man and youth minister. Pat Williamson was Education Director and we had ten children's classes – mostly filled.

We have always believed the heart of the church is the Sunday School where we get to know one another and learn Christian principles first hand. We started in a huge class in room 301 led by Linton Deck, the Superintendent of Orange County Schools. Two of the studies he led were "Gospel of Peanuts" and "The Screwtape Letters." Rick and Lenore Dillard would fill in when Linton was gone.

After Linton left, the class continued and became the Seekers' Class. Chuck Hollingshead, Bill Brown, Pat Brown, Terry Irwin, and occasionally I myself were the teachers.

We moved to Oklahoma for thirteen years but would come back to see our daughter and visit the class. On each return they had moved the class. The class grew smaller because of deaths. Terry Irwin started teaching it and was its mainstay.

We moved back to Winter Park in 2000 and the class had moved again but Terry was still the leader, along with Marilyn Bryant.

Now we're here to stay!

COMPASSION

Compassion Committee

by Kathy Anderson, Chair

Thank you, WPPC for providing me the opportunity to participate in Hands-on-Mission in the local community.

I learned to cook and bake extremely large meals and then participate in the ministry of serving these meals to 350 to 400 homeless people at the Coalition for the Homeless of Central Florida, an outreach program that focuses on offering tools to return homeless people to self-sufficiency. The Coalition is the largest provider of homeless services in Central Florida and the largest residential facility for children an average age of eight years old. I have learned that last year the Coalition provided more than 245,000 nights of shelter, including 79,000 nights of shelter for children, and served more than 300,000 meals. A new men's center opened August 21, 2013.

Sometimes even a simple, smaller meal is prepared for homeless families with children who are temporarily housed at the manse four times a year in participation with The Family Promise of Greater Orlando. Engaging in fellowship during a meal with these families instills a sense of belonging and appreciation. More than eighteen percent of the homeless people in Florida are children and the majority of family households experiencing homelessness are headed by a single parent. The National Alliance to End Homelessness in America reported this year that rent for a two-bedroom apartment in Central Florida is at least $983 *per month.* In order to afford this level of rent and utilities, a household in our area requires 2.4 minimum wage earners working forty hours per week year-round to afford the unit.

Following Hurricane Katrina, which hit in 2005, my son Travis was able to participate and experience disaster recovery aid during two mission trips to the Gulf Coast alongside a team from WPPC. I have learned that Presbyterian Disaster Aid is a key denominational activity.

The Compassion committee offers members of the congregation a bountiful diversity and many more opportunities of ministry to share in Christ's work of compassion, love, and witnessing. I have had the privilege of working with many talented, dedicated, and active members of the Compassion committee, which has been a rewarding and fruitful experience over the past four years. The committee is responsible for mission work, both local and foreign, and the study of mission and social issues.

The PC(USA) World Mission has almost 200 mission workers in more than fifty countries that have been sent around the world continuously since 1837. World Mission addresses the root causes of poverty, especially as it impacts women and children. It also works to share the good news of Jesus Christ and for reconciliation among cultures of violence, including our own.

I am thankful for members of the congregation who have provided me the encouragement to participate over the years in service on other committees of WPPC such as Hannah Circle, Presbyterian Women, Community Life, Personnel, and Budget/Finance. Being a member of WPPC has been a growth experience both spiritually and educationally, and it has enriched my life profoundly.

An IHN Night to Remember

by Richard Small
former IHN Coordinator for WPPC

WPPC was one of the eight charter congregations in the Greater Orlando Area that started up the Interfaith Hospitality Network (IHN) program in Central Florida in 2001.

The network now consists of about twenty congregations, with twelve of them acting in a host capacity. I served as an IHN volunteer and coordinator at WPPC in the late 2000s and early 2010s. No outreach program at WPPC has been dearer to me. Pulling as many as four families at a time back from the abyss of homelessness and giving them lodging, food, security, and friendship as the Family Promise organization counseled them, steered them toward jobs and permanent housing, transported them, and assisted them in so many other ways, was as "hands-on" an outreach activity as I had ever participated in.

WPPC was fortunate in being the only IHN congregation with a dwelling – our manse – an old but still serviceable four-bedroom house that served perfectly as a home for up to four families. WPPC conducts four to five weekly rotations a year. Altogether, the network provides these benefits 365 days a year. That's nonstop.

It didn't take me long to realize that there were many details involved in running this program. Think of the complications you have, or once had, in raising your own family. Multiply that by up to four families. It required forty to fifty volunteers each time we hosted for a week. Of course, we organized and we communicated. Still, there were always surprises. We had some long nights, but we managed.

I cannot help but remember one night in which the surprises seemed to be running on steroids. It was a Sunday night, the first night of a rotation. As coordinator, I liked to welcome the guests on that first night, serve dinner, and stay overnight. On this night (as with many others), my brother-in-law, Matt Straub, served with me. Other than a very light rain at 5:30 p.m., we were ready for a full house – four families, including at least one baby requiring a crib.

When April Chestnut, Family Promise's Case Manager, arrived with several IHN parents in tow and a toddler in her arms, she looked me square in the eye and said, "We've got problems! One family is in ORMC's ER and I'm taking this baby (the one in her arms, who had a fever) to Winter Park ER right now." The mother of the family at ORMC had suffered an allergic reaction to some food. She was expected to be okay, but she had no transportation to WPPC other than by Lynx bus, and she had never been here before. The Winter Park ER family would be transported back to the manse by a third family with a car. Only one of the four families was actually at the manse. We realized by this time that two cribs – not one – would be required. No problem. We had a second crib that we could set up.

As night fell, the rain increased to notable fury. As Matt and I wondered when and exactly how the other three families would arrive, presumably hungry and probably wet, Matt served dinner to the one family while I brought out the second crib, confident that setting it up would be duck soup. Not so. The side designed to be raised and lowered was jammed in the lower position, and no amount of force or magic that these two grown men could bring to bear would change that. So we turned that side to the wall and hoped that the ER mother would be able to deal with it. One little aggravation adding to this part of the ordeal was that one mother, after inspecting the kitchen and reorganizing some of the canned foods, reported back several times (as Matt and I labored on the defective crib) that she had really hoped for bottled water. That kind of attitude among IHN parents rarely surfaces. But we are all human, and besides, this was the night of nights.

At about 9:00 p.m., the ORMC family called from a Lakemont bus stop. Matt, hoping he understood their correct location, took his van out in the now-pouring rain to find and retrieve them. The mother, it turned out, was okay. Half an hour later the two Winter Park ER families (one serving as transportation for the other) arrived as well. The sick baby, now on an antibiotic, was better and yes, the crib arrangement would be fine. By 10:30p.m. we had finished feeding the last of the four families. Soon thereafter the house settled down for the night, and so did the weather. Amazing, we thought, that it all came together.

Matt and I often recollect our experience that night, and we will never forget April's opening exclamation, "We've got problems!" We both love the program and continue to volunteer. The defective bed was replaced. And we still like Sunday nights – usually.

Coalition for the Homeless

by Carla Gehrig

Coalition for the Homeless of Central Florida was created in 1987 by a group of concerned citizens who noted a growing problem of homelessness in the community. This 501(c)(3) nonprofit organization has grown into the largest provider of homeless services in Central Florida and the largest residential facility for children. This past year, the Coalition provided services to nearly 650 people on an average night. Included in that number are nearly 200 children, whose average age is eight, and about one hundred families.

The Coalition has made great strides, expanding its resources, services, and community support. It has grown from a church-outreach to a full-service agency, which now provides food, shelter, housing options, education, advocacy, support services, comprehensive children's services, and case management – all focused on returning homeless men, women, and children to self-sufficiency.

Winter Park Presbyterian Church had been involved in a feeding ministry even before the Coalition was created in 1987. Sometime in the early 1990s, WPPC formed a partnership with the Coalition and we began preparing and serving meals the fourth Friday of every month. We partner this meal with another church – one month they do an entrée and we do a seven-layer salad and the next they might do a salad or vegetable casserole and we do a beef-and-pasta entrée. WPPC provides the milk and lemonade for the meal and the plastic plates, napkins, and flatware.

We fix bagged PB&J sandwiches for the guests to take for consumption the next day along with bagged brownies to be eaten that night or the next day. The same is true of breads/desserts that are donated by Panera each month. To top it off, they are given a bag of toiletries and other items such as a washcloth and sox (both very popular) and all donated by our congregation. And we bring books and magazines that are free for the taking.

We need a minimum of forty volunteers to put smiles on the faces of the 400 guests we will serve. Before meal preparation and serving can begin we must place an insert in the bulletins, do an inventory, order and pick up supplies, and identify volunteers including van and bus drivers as well asservers. Food preparation begins on Thursday and on Friday the food prep is completed and the toiletries sorted and bagged. Everything, including volunteers, is now loaded on vans and the bus.

Now, the fun begins and joy fills our hearts.

Habitat for Humanity

by Mary Beardall

When the story of Winter Park Presbyterian's Habitat involvement is told, the fact that commonly gets left out is that the week before the 1993 PC(USA) General Assembly began, five Habitat houses were started through the Orlando Habitat for Humanity (HFH) Affiliates. Delegates to the General Assembly were encouraged to come early and put in a week's work on this community-wide venture. This was instigated by the Reverend Tom Jones, who felt that GA should leave behind in the community where it met something other than waste paper.

At the urging of Bob Gray, WPPC Interim Pastor, one of these five houses was funded entirely by WPPC, and WPPC volunteers did much of the work on the one we sponsored. The following year (1994) the Winter Park/Maitland Habitat for Humanity Affiliate was formed, so the next four houses WPPC built and paid for were under the WP/Maitland HFH Affiliate auspices. These four houses were built between 1994 and 1998. While WPPC made real efforts to enlist neighborhood churches and volunteers to work with us, the cost was borne entirely by WPPC.

My memory is that we finished the fifth house with a balance of something like $137 in the HFH account and quite a lot of very happy memories. Ray Cook, Steve Schoene, Lee Hall, Chris Rudolph, and Dick and Jean Fuquay carried much of the supervisory and support activities.

Originally, at the behest of Bob Gray and later under Pastor Larry Cuthill's leadership, the whole church became very much involved. The WP/Maitland Affiliate continues to do good work in the community.

Compassion Committee

by Mary Van Hook

Serving on the Compassion Committee gives one a revealing window into the wide variety of outreach efforts at WPPC. It is also a reminder that the church exists not only for its members but also to extend a ministry of concern to a wider community and especially to those in need.

During the meetings, we visit each of the outreach ministries of the church. As a result, our thoughts go to the next mission trip being planned (perhaps to Haiti or Mexico); the CROP walk to address hunger; Family Promise to help homeless families get back on their feet; Coalition to provide food and encouragement for homeless individuals; the Global Market that enables many nonprofit organizations to earn essential funds to carry out their work and income for artisans in other countries; Heifer International that provides animals to assist families; the toy project that enables economically challenged families to give their children Christmas toys in a manner that protects their dignity; and Society for Saint Andrew that organizes gleaning opportunities to help needy families and provides new white socks for homeless individuals.

As members of the committee, we assume the responsibility for coordinating these programs and thus engaging the wider church community in helping to implement them. We also learn about the current activities and challenges facing the WPPC-supported missionaries, who are engaged in a wide variety of activities in many parts of the world. We are reminded of the struggles facing many that are addressed by the special offerings.

As a result, serving on the Compassion Committee serves to expand our vision of the church as well as making us grateful to be in a position to be of service to others. The words, "Inasmuch as ye have done it unto one of the least of these my brethren, ye have done it unto me," are writ large during the Compassion Committee meetings.

Family Promise

by Carla Gehrig

WPPC has been really proud of its long-standing service to Family Promise (formerly Interfaith Hospitality Network [IHN]). Sometimes we have slipped up – but not without humor attached. We are always prompt in providing training to new volunteers, especially if the interest is shortly before a week we are to host.

One time a fairly young couple had just started coming to WPPC for services and were not yet members. They saw a blurb in the *Bulletin* about Family Promise coming up. Their parents had been WPPC members for some time, so they asked them if this was one of the activities they had heard about and could they participate if they were not yet members. Mom said they could but first would have to be trained, and there would be a training session that Sunday in the Parlor of the Christian Education (CE) building.

They signed up for the training and Mom agreed to show them where the CE building and Parlor were located. They were thrilled with the training and tickled to announce to the delighted parents that they would do two nights (8:30 p.m. to 7:30 a.m.). This is the most difficult shift to fill but the best for their working hours.

At 8:25 p.m. their first night, Mom received a frantic call, "Where is the manse? The building is locked up tight, no lights on and no cars. We have walked around all the buildings and they are the same way." They were directed to "look down the street toward the soccer field to the house at the end of the street – that is the manse."

They knew that their training had been at the Parlor and that building also had a kitchen and bathrooms, and they could see other rooms down the hall, so they assumed *that* was the manse. Easily solved and Mom still giggles.

Heifer Project

by Kathy Anderson

For the first time, this year I had the pleasure of volunteering for Vacation Bible School and was delighted to greet the enthusiastic children in the morning and then help with snacks and crafts during the week.

A goal of the Compassion committee this year was realized by supporting a Heifer International project during a mission segment in the VBS program. With training provided by Sue Rudolph, Matt Straub, and Reta Jackson, we found that the children were eager to contribute their allowances and money they had earned by doing chores to fund the purchase of five goats in this year's project, "Goats Give Back," for Nepal.

Since 1987, WPPC has had an extraordinary opportunity to help Heifer International change the world. Last year WPPC received recognition for giving a fifth Ark to Heifer. Each ark represents a donation of $5,000.

Heifer uses these funds to give animals to people in need and to train people in caring for them. Offspring of these animals are then given to others in the community. These donations make a profound difference in the lives of needy families.

White Socks

by Sue Rudolph

I started the white socks drive one year while I was chair of the Coalition for the Homeless. We wanted to collect something at Christmastime that we could give to each client. I know how much the homeless need new socks, so we started this drive. It was probably a good twenty years ago.

So for the past twenty years, I have chaired the campaign.

The people at WPPC are so generous that they usually give enough socks that we can not only give them at Christmas, but we save the rest and give them again – usually in January or February.

Such a small thing to us, but such a big one to men living on the streets, those who sorely need clean and dry socks.

Compassion Ministries

by Carol Howell

I first joined Winter Park Presbyterian Church back in the late 1980s or early 1990s after Betty Messina invited me to take the Bethel Bible Series with her. Chub taught this course for two years and he really inspired me to join the church. I served on both the Finance and Personnel committees.

In March of 1998 I moved to Charlotte, North Carolina for twelve years and transferred my letter to Quail Hollow Presbyterian Church, where I became very active in the Finance Committee and served as an Elder.

In January of 2010 I returned to the Orlando area and transferred my letter back to Winter Park Presbyterian Church. This time I felt I wanted to do something different so I joined the Compassion Committee where I have really enjoyed helping with the preparation of meals for the Coalition for the Homeless once a month.

I have recently begun volunteering for meal preparation for Family Promise and completed training for the Stephen Ministry.

I also oversee all the Special Collections sponsored by Winter Park Presbyterian Church, which include One Great Hour of Sharing during the season of Lent; Caring for

Generations on Easter Sunday; Pentecost Offering received in the season leading up to the Day of Pentecost; Peacemaking Offering received on World Communion Sunday; the Christmas Joy Offering received during Advent; and the Two-Cents-a-Meal offering received once each quarter.

The Two-Cents-a-Meal offering partners with missions fighting hunger throughout the world as well as locally. Current partners are the Second Harvest Food Bank of Central Florida; Society of St. Andrew (which is also here in Florida); the Biblical Basis for Hunger in Haiti; A.I.R. (Alliance for Reforestation), Guatemala; and the Turks who are planting and educating about fruit trees in Madagascar.

Working with the wonderful, caring people of Winter Park Presbyterian Church and helping with the Lord's work is very fulfilling.

Crop Walk

by Sue Rudolph

The Crop Walk is a fund-raiser sponsored by Church World Service – it is a walk for hunger. They have similar walks all over the United States, and it is their principal fund-raiser.

WPPC has participated for some twenty-five years, as a project of the Compassion committee. Originally there was only one big walk in Orlando, and all the churches in Winter Park and Orlando walked together. Later they started a walk just in Winter Park and it was hosted by St. Margaret Mary for several years. Then the Winter Park Congregational

Church stepped in and handled it for a few years, and about five years ago WPPC started hosting it.

I chaired it for a number of years and when I retired, Julie Rankin and George Campbell took it on. George loved it and we regret that he can't chair it anymore. He still participates in his wheel chair, and three people take turns assisting him.

MISSION

WPPC Mission Trips: 1994-2003

by Mary Beardall

In 2003, we observed the tenth year in which mission teams had been going out from Winter Park Presbyterian Church. In the years between 1994 and 1998, these trips lasted ten days to two weeks, and we often visited more than one country, seeking to understand other cultures and the role of the Church in Central America and Peru – what Dr. Cuthill sometimes called "Christian tourism." In the earlier years, contacts were made mostly through ecumenical Christian organizations supported by the PC(USA), such as CEPAD in Nicaragua and CEDEPCA in Guatemala.

As travel costs mounted and more opportunities became available to do useful work alongside new friends in the countries we visited, each trip began to focus on shorter visits to only one country. As a result, from 1999 through 2003, WPPC sent out as many as two or three different groups each summer.

WPPC has been blessed with good friends in each of the countries we have visited. These friends have helped WPPC teams perform useful work while having priceless learning experiences.

1994 WPPC mission team visited Nicaragua. First we toured Managua, led by CEPAD (an extension of PC(USA) Worldwide Mission). We joined in construction work and Bible school at La Finca (the farm and conference site near Matagalpa being developed by Young Life in Nicaragua under the direction of Jim and Sara Hornsby). This was followed by a tour of Guatemala City and Chimaltenango, Guatemala with CEDEPCA, the Guatemala representative of PC(USA) Worldwide Mission.

1995 WPPC's first visit to Peru, where we were hosted by Paul and Marty Clark of Scripture Union (SU) in Lima and crossed the spectacular Andes Mountains to visit Kimo, one of the sites where SU resettles the boys they have rescued from the streets of Lima. We also visited mission sites of the Peruvian Presbyterian Church in Lima. Then we revisited PC(USA) mission sites in Guatemala, and Young Life sites in Nicaragua, doing construction work and conducting a Bible school at La Finca.

1996 We returned to Peru to work with Scripture Union in Lima and at Kimo, followed by a return to Nicaragua (construction work at La Finca and for the wedding of Martina and Emerson Wilson, WPPC member/missionaries). We also conducted Bible schools at Kimo, Peru and at La Finca, Nicaragua.We flew to Lima and then across the Andes to Iquitos, Peru's major town in the Amazon River basin, to do construction work and conduct a Bible school at Puerto Alegria, an SU orphanage in the jungle near Iquitos.

1997 WPPC mission teams returned to Peru for continued construction work and Bible school with SU at Iquitos and Puerto Alegria. In addition, John and Carla Gehrig, Linda Kirk, and Meg Ball introduced WPPC Mission Teams to what can be done through distributing free eyeglasses For the first time, the mission team's work included distribution of Volunteer Optometric Service to Humanity (VOSH) eye glasses.

1998 WPPC did three mission trips this year: (1) to Chimaltenango, Guatemala, with A.I.R. (Alliance for International Reforestation) and VOSH; (2) construction work and Bible School at Kawai, SU's campsite and group home on the Pacific Ocean just south of Lima, Peru; and (3) construction, Bible School, and VOSH at Puerto Alegria, Iquitos, Peru.

2000 Three mission trips again this year: (1) in Chimaltenango, Guatemala: with A.I.R., laying the foundations for a new office building, Bible school, and home visits; VOSH clinic; (2) scouting trip to Nogales, AZ/Sonora, MX with our own Mary Kinney, a volunteer in mission with PC(USA) Border Ministry. Mary arranged for WPPC mission teams to work, learn, and serve at Border Ministry sites in Nogales, AZ / Nogales, MX; (3) construction and Bible School with SU in Peru at Kawai; and (4) with SU in Peru (Iquitos/Puerto Alegria – construction, Bible school, and VOSH).

2001 Again, three mission trips: (1) in Chimaltenango, Guatemala, completion of the A.I.R. office building; (2) with Mary Kinney in Nogales AZ/Sonora, MX: a VOSH clinic, construction, and Bible school; and (3) in Peru with SU at Kimo, construction, Bible school, and VOSH clinic.

2002 (1) First mission trip to Cuba, arranged with Rachel Cardonas of the Reformed Church of Cuba; the interdenominational seminary in Matanzas (the Bush administration had temporarily lifted its ban on religious and educational travel to Cuba – since rescinded); (2) in Nicaragua, VOSH clinics in Matagalpa and at La Finca: construction and Bible school at La Finca; and (3) WPPC's first mission trip to Brazil: travel by boat up the River Negro in the Amazon River basin with both the Manaus Presbyterian Church and VOSH.

2003 Three mission trips again this year: (1) Bible school and construction projects in Juarez, MX, arranged by Mary Kinney and the PC(USA) Border Ministry; (2) return to Matagalpa, Cuba; and (3) return to Peru to help SU build a resettlement home for street boys north of Lima near Yungay; construction, Bible school, and a VOSH clinic.

On these mission trips, WPPC members are frequently joined by other Presbyterians from throughout the Presbytery, and often by individuals from other denominations. The trips were the long-time vision of then-WPPC senior pastor, Larry Cuthill, who taught that by getting outside our comfort zone we can see ourselves and our place in God's world more clearly. Whatever work that mission team members are able to accomplish is good, but it is nowhere nearly as important as what the mission-team experience is able to do foreach individual. We formed relationships with some of God's children who are outside of our everyday circle of family, friends, and coworkers.

In addition to those who have actually traveled abroad, many WPPC members have added their prayers and their financial assistance, and have provided materials used for Bible school. Much of the WPPC mission story lies in the value accrued to those who remain at home. In this way the plight of a child abandoned on the street of Lima, the impoverished farmer whose hillside is stripped bare by deforestation in Guatemala, the young person hungry to know Christ in Nicaragua becomes more real to those worshiping in the pews at WPPC. By their many contributions – e.g., crayons, scissors, and other supplies for jungle Bible Schools, unused eyeglasses, building materials, prayers for the groups and for individuals, financial support, sewing clothes for children – the congregation of WPPC has made itself as much a part of the Mission Teams as those who have mounted the steps of the airplane.

WPPC Mission Trips: 2004 – 2013

by John Gehrig

By 2004, many of the experienced missioners from WPPC had participated in the eye clinic teams, which functioned as a part of the church mission trips. All of those who had so participated found the eye clinics very worthwhile, both for themselves and for the team's patients. As a result, most of the WPPC mission trips began to focus on team work as a principal mission activity of the eye-care team, while many others on the mission team continued to work on construction projects and Bible school activities.

2004 WPPC's mission trip this year was to Ica, Peru. We were sponsored once again by Scripture Union and worked at their facility in Ica with Billy Clark, son of founders Paul and Marty Clark. Ica is a hot, extremely dry desert town and living and working there was an amazing experience for us. We saw more than 1,000 adult patients and about 100 orphanage children. We were able to equip almost all of them with suitable glasses and we had many "Aha" moments.

2005 WPPC returned to Peru for another rewarding mission team experience with Scripture Union and yet another eye clinic. Later in the year, our mission team headed for Romania with a pastor from Orlando Baptist Church and worked on a medical/vision mission with the Roma people (gypsies) in a small town in Eastern Romania. This was truly a unique experience. We were told that we were the first church team *ever* to work with the gypsies in Romania.

2006 The year of Hurricane Katrina – WPPC mission teams responded in true style, mounting relief and reconstruction efforts in Bay St. Louis and Waveland, Mississippi. Reverend George Campbell, our Parish Associate, showed us and our church the way when he joined Presbyterian Disaster Assistance (PDA) immediately after the hurricane and helped establish and then became the Director of the huge PDA volunteer camp in D'Iberville, Miss.

2007 Hurricane Katrina Relief in full swing – WPPC sent three mission teams to the Relief Worker's camp in D'Iberville where they joined hundreds of other Christian relief workers in rebuilding D'Iberville through clean-up and reconstruction efforts.

2008 One small mission team went to the Ukraine to work with Reverend Bob Gamble, a former WPPC associate pastor, at his project in Odessa, "This Child Here." Reverend Bob's project is a shelter-and-sustenance center for street children. There are more than a thousand street children in Odessa, living in abandoned factories, tunnels, sewers, and outdoors. We were truly able to see God's grace at work. Audrey Ball, one of our team members, was so inspired by this trip that she retired from teaching in Seminole County and has since dedicated her life to ministering to the orphans of Odessa. A large team went to Arequipa, Peru, where we were sponsored by the Presbyterian Church of Arequipa. We worked withthat church, a Korean Presbyterian mission, and two Pentecostal churches during the four days of our eye clinics, spending two days at each of the sites, and we were able to see more than 1,500 patients.

2009 The WPPC mission team returned to Arequipa to work with the Presbyterian Church there, and in addition to our now traditional eye clinic, teams engaged in extensive heavy construction projects – rehabilitating a police orphanage for children whose parental rights had been terminated due to neglect, digging a huge septic tank and drainage field, replumbing a Pentecostal church, and laying a new tile patio for our host church.

2010 WPPC returned to our partner Presbyterian Church in Arequipa, this time for the third straight year, and conducted another eye-care clinic, this time featuring new eye glasses made on the site by Peruvian optometrists who had "adopted" us on previous trips.

2011 WPPC made its first mission trip to Haiti, sponsored by Haiti Outreach Missions, a group that operates three church-school compounds in the Port-Au-Prince area. The principal compound is in *Cite Soleil*, the largest slum in Haiti. We conducted eye clinics at each compound and a construction team worked on the school facilities in *Cite Soleil*.

2012 WPPC returned to Haiti, working this time in *Leogane* with the Episcopal Church, which maintains the famous *Leogane* hospital supported by the Presbyterian Medical Benevolence Foundation. *Leogane* had just been hit by yet another hurricane and we were able to bring eye-care assistance to more than one thousand adults and children.

2013 Matt Pickler, a child of WPPC and a Peace Corps worker based in Guadalajara, Mexico, organized a week-long eye-care mission that was based in nearby *Colcula* and in *Camichines*, a neighboring farm town. Our two clinics were based at an orphanage in *Camichines* supported by the Presbyterian Church in Guadalajara and at a reformed Protestant church in *Colcula*. We saw more than eight hundred patients and all our exam fees from the clinic were donated to the orphanage.

We look forward to many years of helpful Christian service to our brothers and sisters everywhere. More important, we look forward to spiritual sharing and growth in the Word with them.

From Odessa, With Love

by Audrey Ball

A memory, write about a single memory, was the invitation. I have so many fond thoughts of Winter Park Presbyterian Church that it seems impossible to write about just one.

WPPC was the haven I found when I moved to Florida twenty-three years ago. I had spent the entirety of my life up to that point in small rural towns in southeast Pennsylvania, and suddenly here I was in the suburbs of Orlando. New city, new home, new job in a new school (I am a teacher) – new everything it seemed. In many ways I felt as if I had moved to a new planet, not just a new state. I visited churches in the first weeks that I was here, trying to ground myself and looking for "home."I found it at WPPC. I was no longer alone in a new place.

WPPC nurtured me, and my life became more and more centered here in the church. I taught Sunday School and Vacation Bible School, served on a variety of committees, and as a Deacon and a Session member. I ushered and greeted. I worked, played, and prayed there. And I went on my first mission trip. It was to Nogales, Mexico, to help with a VOSH eye clinic. Later, in Katrina's aftermath, I went to rebuild houses in D'Iberville, Mississippi. Finally, I traveled to Odessa, Ukraine, to learn more about the problem of parentless, homeless children. And I believe that it is because of those trips that I am where I am today, and that will be my "single memory."

Today, my life is a mission trip. I live and work in Odessa. After that first trip, I came home in body, but not entirely in spirit. That initial peek at children living on the streets and languishing in orphanages made it impossible for me to go back to living my tidy, comfortable little life in America. Still, I needed nine months to reflect and to pray and to figure how it could be possible for me to go alone to this strange place called Odessa, Ukraine, and to stay a while to work with children who had no one. In due time, God removed all the obstacles, and my plan to come here was realized. Still, as I was readying for this very personal, very solitary mission, I once again felt very alone.

And once again, I became wrapped in the arms of this very loving and giving church. Not once in all the years I've been here have I ever again felt alone. WPPC sent me off with prayers and gifts and good wishes. WPPC has remained here with me through thick and thin, spiritually and tangibly. My plan was to stay for one year. I've stayed for five now. Through those years, *together*, we have established a small and personal program for

graduates of orphanages. They are fed, clothed, nurtured physically and spiritually, mentored in the skills of independent living and, most of all, they are loved. It may be me who is physically present here, but WPPC is the greatest part of this mission.

I am humbled and grateful to be a member of this body of Christ, Winter Park Presbyterian Church, the church that makes it possible to "go into the world" and to "care for orphans."

Accompaniers in Guatemala

by Mary Beardall

In 1994 when Dr. Cuthill first suggested that members from WPPC might visit PC(USA) Mission sites in Nicaragua and Guatemala, I had two reservations: I was neither at all clear about (1) exactly where either country was on the map nor (2) what he meant by "mission." If that term meant that we, as better-informed Americans, were going to go somewhere to twist the arms of the "natives" to our understanding of Christ's gospel, then neither Bill nor I wanted any part of it.

That, of course, turned out to be a completely inaccurate vision of the groups' intentions. We discovered from a map that both Nicaragua and Guatemala are in Central America just south of Mexico, and that a WPPC Mission Team would be seeking to understand better our Christian (and non-Christian) brothers and sisters living nearby in cultures vastly, though not entirely, different from our own, and to offer them whatever practical help might lie in our power to provide.

In the summer of 1994 and again in 1995, Bill and I were part of the WPPC Mission Teams that visited and worked with PC(USA) Mission sites in Guatemala, a country then in the midst of a horrifyingly violent civil war, caused in part by actions that had been taken in the past by both the U.S. government and by U.S. commercial interests. We found among our PC(USA) mission contacts some genuinely compelling Christian friends, and we had close contact with fellow Christians who had suffered deeply during Guatemala's brutal civil war.

By 1995, United Nations Peacemakers had made some progress in resolving the situation (under UN auspices, a Peace Treaty had been signed in December of 1995) but the Presbyterian Worldwide Mission division continued to be very worried about the safety of Guatemalan Presbyterians (Latino *and* Quiche*). For some time, the Worldwide Mission office had been recruiting North American Presbyterians to become "accompaniers" to Presbyterian mission ventures (churches, schools, and such). I signed up to become an accompanier for a month, much to the astonishment of my husband, my pastor, and my children. (My children never got over the idea that I would somehow be standing in the doorway fending off in-coming fire.)

In early January of 1996 I flew off to Guatemala, becoming more trepidatious as departure time grew nearer. But except for the inconveniences of living in a Sunday School classroom in a minimally furnished Central American church, speaking and understanding very little Spanish, and inevitable loneliness, the most frightening thing about the trip was riding along the Pan American Highway from Guatemala City north to Quetzeltenango (known locally as "Xela") in a car driven by a very inexperienced but very enthusiastic young man who worked for the Presbytery. At the end of my month-long commitment I arranged for a professional courier to take me from Quetzeltenango to Ann Hallum'sA.I.R. office in Chimaltenango.

Besides being "a presence" in the Xela Presbyterian Church – whose Quiche pastor, anxious to emphasize his Presbyterian orthodoxy, made frequent references in his sermons to the teachings of "Juan Calvino"—my main task was to be "a presence" at the La Patria Presbyterian School. La Patria is a well-established, highly successful Presbyterian boarding and day school with an excellent academic reputation. During the weeks I was there, it seemed that my most useful contribution was to sit in on the English classes and pronounce the vocabulary words. If you ever meet young Guatemalan adults from the northwest part of the country who speak English with a Southern accent you will know where they got it.

I had wonderful Christian and educational experiences in the Church and at La Patria. I never encountered any in-coming fire (although there were many, many UN vehicles patrolling the streets). But I did get to know some wonderful Christians, both Latino and Quiche, who had survived the years of "the Violencia," Guatemala's Civil War.

Quiche is a Mayan linguistic group.

MUSIC

Chancel Choir Days

by Jodi Tassos

When I moved to Florida in 1971, I joined Winter Park Presbyterian Church and the choir. Walter Hewitt was the organist and director of music at that time. There were six choirs: Training, Chapel Boys, Chapel Girls, Junior High, High School, and Chancel. Walter was a brilliant organist and highly organized. Before moving to Florida, he had played at a large church in New Jersey and was a full-time, professional church musician. When he retired from our church, he soon discovered he needed to continue being involved with church music and for several years was the organist at the First Methodist Church in Winter Park.

After Walter left, finding a comparable musician was a challenge. Steven Farrell had a very brief tenure as organist/choir director. When the committee met to discuss his short-comings, Dr. Delgado even questioned whether we were suffering from a "Rebecca" complex, referring to Daphne duMaurier's novel.

If memory serves me correctly, our next choir director was Ty Riddle. Ty did not play the organ and we had several different organists at that time: Kathy Atkisson, Helen Baker, and Kay Edwards, all excellent musicians.

Sometime in the early 1980s Dr. Richard Winchell, a composer, became our choir director and his wife Julie Winchell the organist. Both were very gifted musicians. My fondest memory during their tenure was the production of *Amahl and the Night Visitors* that the choir performed. Their two oldest children, Kate and John, shared the role of Amahl, and we did two performances so each could sing it. I had the pleasure of singing the role of Mother and it was both a musically and spiritually rewarding experience. The Winchells moved to Cape Cod.

Dana Irwin, our next director, held our choir together during a difficult transition and built up the bell choir. There were two organists during Dana's ten-year tenure, Liz Jennings and Joanna Wallace.

Our next leader was Randy Day, a gifted musician, who was both organist and choir director. The organ was repositioned in front of the choir so he could conduct from the console. Randy is now a church musician in Pennsylvania.

Trey Jacobs, choral director at Winter Park High School, became our next director. At times he set the bar higher than our skills could achieve, which gave him considerable frustration. But again, the spirit of the choir prevailed.

We were blessed when Dr. Al Holcomb took over the choir and brought both choral skills and spiritual meaning to the responsibility. And who can ever forget Organist George Grace, whose ebullient personality reminded us to never take ourselves too seriously.

Justin Chase has continued that combination of choral excellence and spiritual depth. Our most recent addition to the music program, following Joe Ritchie, is the talented organist, Bill Kent.

Saga of the Reuter's Organ

by Dick Sturm

Thanks to all the efforts of Jim Leach and his tenacity that started about eleven years before, we were able to order our organ.

I remember – and can still see him in my mind's eye – standing in the narthex in his choir robe with a big organ pipe in his efforts to promote the fact that we needed a new organ!

Joanna Wallace was our organist when I was approached by Dr. Cuthill to head up the fund-raising committee. In the course of events, the selection committee traveled to several different churches, listening to and viewing different instruments in Orlando, but also as far afield as Fort Lauderdale, and Saint Petersburg. The travels were enjoyable and they even included complimentary lunches on some occasions. We listened and observed and finally decided on a pipe organ (about which, by the way, some of our major donors were very adamant).

We started our fund-raising with a goal of $460,000, which was the cost of our new instrument. We made personal visits to our members during the next few weeks explaining our need. Joanna underscored the need by demonstrating the lack of certain keys on our current instrument. The keys were there but they didn't work. Our old organ, I believe, was not economically repairable.

After receiving the necessary pledges, the organ was ordered and then delivered to a waiting crowd of members in the west parking lot Monday, September 21, 1998. We unloaded more than 3,000 pipes, some in boxes, others handled with kid gloves so as not to tarnish or damage them between the truck and Fellowship Hall. When we had finished unloading, the Hall looked like a disaster zone.

The fellow that sold us the organ also directed the unloading of the truck and then proceeded to do the installation.

Our organ was dedicated November 21, 1998, with a concert by noted organist John Walker, much to the delight of the entire congregation.

To celebrate the completion of this enormous project, a special arrangement of "Holy, Holy, Holy" was presented to Jim Leach in appreciation of his efforts in this matter over the years.

Winter Park Music

by Susan and Alan Davis

We started attending WPPC in the fall of 2005. I had been hired to direct children's music, and we both soon got involved in the Westminster Ringers and the Chancel Choir, directed by Al Holcomb.

In the next few years, I learned so much about choral music from Al and from other gifted singers in the choir. I also learned a lot about working with people by observing Al's leadership style. We began to find our niche in a musical ensemble of wonderful, caring people.

George Grace agreed to accompany the Children's Choir, and I immediately realized how fortunate I was to have the support and assistance of such a gifted musician as George. Besides accompanying the children superbly, he always kept our rehearsals fun by interjecting his own brand of humor. The children loved him, as did I.

Through the next few years, I watched as children grew up in our Children's Choir program. This year, children who started with us as kindergarteners have "graduated" to seventh grade and middle school. It has been such a pleasure to see these precious little children grow into kind and caring youth, as well as good singers and actors.

When Al and George moved to Princeton, I wondered how anyone could possibly fill their shoes, because it is so hard to follow in the footsteps of beloved leaders. Amazingly enough, we found that we had a superb director sitting in the midst of the Chancel Choir, and Justin Chase accepted the position of Director of Music at WPPC.

Because the position of handbell director was also vacant, I stepped in to fill that spot. Joe Ritchie took George Grace's place as organist/accompanist, and he also graciously agreed to accompany the Children's Choir.

When Joe took a job in another state the following year, we were again blessed to find a gifted and patient accompanist in Bill Kent.

When I first heard the term, Choir Wranglers, I laughed, but very soon I realized that expression fit Nancy Appich and Susie Stone to a T. These sweet ladies, along with Alan, attend all of our rehearsals and lend immeasurable assistance to our program. Our children are surrounded by caring adults and exceptional role models.

Throughout the process of replacing leaders and ensemble members as their tenure with us has ended, I have come to realize that one reason we have been blessed with such wonderful musicians has been because WPPC has always made its music program a priority. Musicians *want* to participate in such a quality program – where everyone truly cares about each other.

But there is more to "church" than the music, isn't there? Over the years, we have come to respect and appreciate the selflessness and maturity of our congregation. People who share a genuine interest in the community of WPPC work tirelessly to promote a sense of home, and *music* is just one of the many components of home.

The Music of the Chancel Choir

by Dana Irwin

Through the years, our Chancel Choir has sung a variety of anthems in many styles from many eras, with texts appropriate for worship. We have also presented larger works for special worship services. The list includes selections from Handel's *Messiah*, cantatas by Buxtehude and Bach, Vivaldi's *Gloria*, Stainer's *Crucifixion*, Pergolesi's *Magnificat*, *A New Creation* by Clausen, and requiems by Faure, Brahms, and Rutter. For the extended works we have been accompanied by organ, small ensemble, or small orchestra. Learning and presenting this music is spiritually rewarding for the choir and truly our gift to God's people in this place.

In the 1980s we collaborated with Park Lake Presbyterian and First Presbyterian of Maitland in a Festival of the Sacred Arts. Each choir worked on the music during its own rehearsals, and then a guest conductor came on the weekend of the festival to work with the combined choirs for the concert on Sunday. Similar, smaller efforts of that nature have been done in recent times, too. It is a joy to join others in this kind of event.

The choir has also stepped out of the choir loft on a number of occasions to entertain the audience with Broadway, movie, and popular music. Those shows were benefits. The first one, in 1981, earned the choir the robes we were still wearing in 2013. Proceeds from other shows went to Habitat for Humanity, the Bonnie Wilhite Music Scholarship Fund, our organ fund, and a small scholarship to one of our members – Roger Sodsod – who was studying for his master's degree in voice.

There are some fun memories from these productions. Jodi Tassos took a very formal tenor soloist and got him to sing "Everything's up to Date in Kansas City" from *Oklahoma* like a true fun-loving cowboy. Jayne Leach made our then-pastor Bob Gray blush by singing, adoringly, to him "Why Can't You Behave?" from *Kiss Me Kate*. Jeanne Vinci and Jerry Clement, coached by Judy Graham, sang the *Guys and Dolls* number "I Love You, a Bushel and a Peck" in a dead-pan style imitating the Grant Wood American Gothic painting. And Judy danced the Charleston with Cindy Nants, Bonnie Wilhite, Glenda Lowrey, and Roger Sodsod. She also did a Fred Astaire number.

Work on these shows was always done after regular choir music was rehearsed, so it was an extra effort by all, but an enjoyable way to let our hair down.

PRESCHOOL

A History of the Preschool Program
1983-1999

The WPPC Preschool was established in 1959. Early Directors were Virginia Bailey, Mary Miller, and Eva Clark.

by Anne Bensinger
former Preschool Director

Years ago, before the public school incorporated kindergarten programs, the Winter Park Presbyterian Church had a kindergarten program for five-year-olds. Many of those students have since become parents and now grandparents of preschool age children. When kindergarten was made mandatory in the public schools, WPPC disbanded its kindergarten in favor of a program for children under kindergarten age.

In 1983, a subcommittee of the Christian Education Committee was established to determine the need for a preschool program for two-, three-, and four-year-olds. The first program enrolled fifty children, began under the direction of Mrs. Evie Park, former founder and first director of the Park Lake Presbyterian Church Preschool and Day Care Center in Orlando, and was called the Winter Park Presbyterian Weekday School.

Weekday School was overseen by the Weekday School Board, which was under the auspices of Christian Education (CE) and its director, Pat Williamson (DCE). The Session of the Church was the ultimate supervisory body, approving the management and work of the School through CE. At this time there was also established a separate Mother's Day Out Program for toddlers directed by Sue Rudolph. The two programs did not share facilities or supplies and were managed independently through CE.

From its inception, the goal of the Weekday School (now called the Winter Park Presbyterian Preschool Program) was to offer excellent early childhood education and Christian child care to both church and to church community member families, and to this date, the goal has remained unchanged.

Initially, the curriculum chosen by CE for the Weekday School was a traditional pre-kindergarten, unit-based preschool curriculum with monthly calendars sent to parents and age-appropriate activities offered to the children by teachers with various backgrounds educationally and experientially. Weekday School was not licensed by HRS or any other licensing agency, as licensing was not yet legislatively mandated for church-sponsored programs.

In 1985, it was determined by Mrs. Park, with approval of the Weekday School Board, CE, and Session, that the Weekday School teachers would take part in training in the High Scope Curriculum being offered to the Orange County Schools through the Orlando Vo-Tech Center. High Scope is a nationally known, used, and revered curriculum based on the work and research of David Welkart of the University of Michigan. Its philosophy is that young children must be given a stimulating, organized environment in which they can actively manipulate a variety of appropriate materials in order to experience optimum development of physical, mental, and social-emotional skills. The most important themes of High Scope are active learning and developmental appropriateness. It was further determined that the Weekday School would continue to offer Christian education experiences and learning in addition to the High Scope curriculum.

In 1989, a consulting report was done by William Alexander, Director of Childcare at the First Presbyterian Church of Orlando, which suggested uses of church space by both Weekday School and Mother's Day Out and how both programs might best be managed and improved, and how enrollment might be increased. In that same year, Mrs. Park retired and Anne Bensinger was hired as director. Weekday School and Mother's Day Out, now under the able directorship of Paige Mercer, were combined to become the Winter Park Presbyterian Preschool Programs.

At this point, the Programs became a single entity with a separate and singular mission, no longer under CE, but functioning with an autonomous Board, reporting directly to Session as any other Church committee.

The Programs were supported financially by the Church in terms of rent-free space and utilities, and administrative support was also provided. Monies remaining in the Programs budget at the end of each year were returned to the Church to offset operating costs. Fundraising efforts were also undertaken in order to purchase special equipment and materials needed by the Programs.

In February 1999, Anne Bensinger retired and Laurel Zinssar was hired as Director; Mrs. Zinssar has remained as Director to the present time.

A History of the Preschool Program
1999 to 2013

by Laurel Zinssar
Preschool Director

The Preschool was initially a very successful nursery school that met the needs of stay-at-home families. The children were able to socialize and enjoy an excellent developmental preschool program. In addition, parents of toddlers were offered a parent's day out. The school had two four-day and one five-day 4-year-old classes, five two-day 4-year-old, four three-day 3-year-old, and two part-time Parents Day Out programs. There were no five-day options for children under the age of 4. In addition we had an extended-day option to attend 8:30 in the morning and 3:00 in the afternoon. The Preschool also had a four-day summer camp that was offered for three weeks. As a Christian program we offered Chapel and a program based on Christian principals. We have steadily worked on improving Chapel and building a program that has specific goals and direction. This objective has been achieved. We also added an art and a music-and-movement program. This allows children to enjoy activities that are no longer offered in early elementary school.

Over the years we have added an additional 4-year-old class that is now part of a state program called Voluntary Pre-K. The quality of the education that the children receive and complying with the new rigorous standards increased the focus from a play-based to a measured educational experience that prepares the children to meet the academic standards of today's kindergarten. In addition, we added an infant room that meets the needs of working parents, many who have children already enrolled in the program.

The Preschool was not computerized in 1999 and the educational requirements for the staff were not as rigorous as those that the current Department of Children and Families now require. There was not a staff room and the supply room was needed for classroom space. Over the years we were able to add a new staff room, supply room, and art room as well as an additional Pre-K classroom. The classroom equipment was also in need of updating. Computerizing the program was an easy first step. This included purchasing computers and a program to manage the children's information as well as using a computer program to keep track of salaries and other financial information.

In order to meet the needs of working families, the Preschool began to offer a five-day program for all ages. In addition the Preschool hours of operation increased to offer care from 8:00 to 3:30. Summer Camp is now offered five days a week for six weeks.

The Florida Department of Children and Families, our governing licensing agency, has considerably increased its educational requirements for working in a licensed preschool. Our staff meets these new requirements. They are better educated and as a result their salaries have gone up. As the years passed it has been necessary to continue to update worn-out materials, supplies, and the outside playground equipment. This has been done over time.

In order to accomplish these goals it was necessary to allow the families to register for more days, increase the hours of operation, offer a longer summer camp, open more classrooms, computerize the school, hire staff with early-childhood-education background, improve the quality of the classroom equipment and materials, and obtain national accreditation.

Changes consist of computerization; adding eight weeks of summer camp; extending the 8:30 to 3:00 day to 8:00 to 3:30; adding a five-day program option for all ages; and adding five new rooms including an art room, two new classrooms, an additional office, work room, and kitchen area. As a result we were able to use added income to compensate the staff for increased education, better compensate the Church, continue to improve the classrooms in order to provide a better learning environment for the children and to stay competitive, and meet the needs of families in changing times by meeting the needs of working parents and employing and keeping an exceptional staff.

Although the Preschool is considered a mission of the church, it was important to make a more realistic contribution to help the Church defer its costs. Over the years the donation has increased to meet this need, and we are now considered one of the best in the area for quality and education.

YOUTH

Youth Programs

by Ginny Seel

The youth programs have always played an important part in the life of the church. Some of the most memorable years, due to the large number of youth involved, were the 1960s, '70s, and '80s. There were full-time ordained Associate Youth Ministers and a Director of Education on staff.

In the 1960s and '70s, there was a program for seventh and eighth graders to prepare them for confirmation. It was a two-year program called Youth Club. The program consisted of four parts: study, recreation, choir, and service. It was so popular with the young people that it became the place to be on a weekday afternoon after school.

Our youth brought their friends and it soon grew to a large group of fifty or so young people. Of course, not all of these became members of the church but they learned a great deal and had a lot of fun. The principal of Howard Junior High School (a member) was sometimes called in to help keep order (and discipline).

At the end of the two years, the eighth graders went on an overnight campout at a local campground. One of the ministers and the Director of Education and chaperones accompanied them. Everyone slept in tents.

The purpose of this outing was to provide an opportunity for each youth to have a one-on-one conversation with the minister about the important step they were considering in becoming a member of Christ's Church and specifically of the Winter Park Presbyterian Church. Of course, there was time for swimming, canoeing, volleyball, water fights, and the like.

Our Director of Christian Education at the time was a lovely, spiritual, fun-loving woman – and the youth loved her. The last afternoon as the youth were helping pack up to leave, the DCE and one of the chaperones decided to take a quick canoe ride. When we came close to shore she said, "Wouldn't the kids get a kick out of us tipping over the canoe?" The chaperone quickly agreed and over it went.

What the chaperone and the minister on shore did not know was that the DCE couldn't swim. Finally realizing that she was not kidding around, the minister quickly swam out and dragged her back to shore. She was laughing the whole time and it is a wonder that there weren't serious consequences. To this day some of the former youth recall the incident and remember the fun it all was. (They would be in their late forties and early fifties now.)

Thirty-three young people confirmed their baptism on Palm Sunday of 1975 and became members of the church. What a glorious year for WPPC and for our faith! Several of those youth went into full-time Christian ministry.

The Living Nativity

by Sue Rudolph

I joined WPPC thirty-four years ago. Our girls were 9 and 12 years of age and they were quickly herded into the Youth Activities by our Director of Christian Education, Pat Williamson. She also asked me if I would like to serve on the Christian Ed Committee and she wasn't taking "No" for an answer!

By far the most popular Christmas activity the youth participated in was the Living Nativity. Pat had arranged this yearly activity and it had become a state-of-the-art pageant. The costuming was fabulous, and our members made all of the costumes.

Pat had connections to the animal world and she got every farm animal known to man for our stable and even convinced the local Shriners to allow their Parade camel to be a part of our Nativity every year. How did Gus come to church? On a bus of course! All the kids were fond of saying, "here comes Gus on the Bus!" Gus was with us until he was very old; the last few years he spent lying down most of the time, and more often than we would have liked, he let out his EXTREMELY *LOUD* **BELLOW**!

We had cows, sheep, a donkey, goats – and Gus. There are lots of stories about escapes that the animals made over the four-day period when they were penned up at the church for the Living Nativity.

My favorite is about the time that our minister, Dr. Delgado, looked out the window of his office and saw the cow standing in the middle of Lakemont! He called Pat Williamson and she ran out to Lakemont and grabbed the cow by the tail! She then waited for a pack of Presbyterians to run out of the church and help her herd the cow back to its pen.

Another year, all of the sheep got out of the pen, and crossed Lakemont into the orange grove area that is now Windsong. Ken Shick, our associate pastor, gathered up a group and they spent quite a while running through the orange groves chasing, catching, and returning the sheep. I think they all came away with more appreciation of what a shepherd's life must have been like!

The Youth Group learned that one had to "earn" a spot in the Nativity. One could only be an age-appropriate character. The very youngest could be shepherds (boys and girls) if they had an adult accompanying them. The next step up for the girls was to be a field angel. Field angels came in a group and announced to the Shepherd's,

Fear not: for, behold, I bring you good tidings of great joy,
which shall be to all people.
For unto you is born this day in the city of David, a Saviour,
which is Christ the Lord.

While listening to this proclamation, the Shepherds (every size) were appropriately awed and scared. They reacted by putting their hands over their heads or fell backwards on the ground or, a few I saw over the years, put their hands over their ears, which of course made it harder to *hear* the proclamation!

The next step for girls was to become the manger angel, the age span for this was around 10 to 13 and all the girls loved standing behind the baby Jesus in the manger with their wings held high. You could almost hear the "Gloria" coming from their mouths.

The most celebrated part, of course, was to be old enough to be Mary. They were very serious about being Mary, and more than one shared with me that when they were Mary, they were filled with the wonder of what that young Mary must have been thinking, looking down at baby Jesus in that manger. There were times over the years when we actually had young mothers and fathers bring their infants. How meaningful it was to those families and to those of us that saw the love they had for their newborn.

The teenage boys were able to be wise men. There was also the part of King Herod, but it was very hard to fill. No one wanted to be King Herod!

Of course the older teen boys were able to play the part of Joseph. I wonder what those boys thought? They must have had many thoughts about the Bible story and how Joseph obeyed God by taking Mary as his wife and trusting God for their future and for the future of this precious baby Jesus.

Over the years, my grandchildren all participated in the Living Nativity and loved it as their parents did.

On the 60th Anniversary of WPPC, it's important to remember the different ways the church has reached out to members and to the community to spread the word of God. We are told to tell the story to every generation. Let's do it!

Memories of WPPC

by Barbara Bowers Linn

My brother and I came here as children and went to church, sang in the choir, and attended Vacation Bible School from 1958 through 1965. We lived at 1870 Carollee Lane and crossed the vacant field to come to church every Sunday.

I have very fond memories. We visit here every year

Youth Group

by Betty Hines

When our youngest son Robert was in the youth group (in the early 1980s), they would go on field trips to Wekiwa Springs on a big bus. Dr. Glenn Bass and Dr. Ken Shick would go with them. After swimming and other activities they would all gather round in a group. Both Glenn and Ken would bring their guitars with them and they all had a fabulous time singing lots and lots of songs.

Ty Riddle was the Music Director at that time and he thought it would be a good idea if all the WPPC students who were in the Glenridge Junior High School band would start practicing some of the anthems and then would accompany the choir. The end result made a fabulous hit with all who heard it and the band members will still remember it. Ty was asked to take a few of the band with him when he was asked to play at another church. Also – a big hit!

A bunch of the same group loved taking part in the Living Nativity. They would take turns playing different roles. They loved teasing the animals and got along well with all except – the *camel*!

Memories of WPPC

by Rachel LaRue Freeman

Hello. My name is Rachel LaRue Freeman. I am a daughter of Marianna and Roger LaRue – long-time members of WPPC. I was actually baptized at WPPC by Dr.

Delgado in 1964-65. My parents brought me and my siblings (Marguerite and Patrick) to the church for just about everything when we were growing up. I even attended kindergarten there.

I remember the church being a fun place with lots of activities and energy. I was in the children's choir for years when Sir was the director. He had white, closely cropped hair and black thick glasses. He was not tall, but he was tall to us when we were little. I recall him driving a white Ford Mustang and it struck me as a pretty hip and sporty car for a church choir director. Sir always expected the best out of us and rehearsed us to earn high marks with our singing. When it was time to actually sing in church, we knew that we were ready. I recall being amazed with the voice of Virginia Murchison in the adult choir as a child. She'd blast out the notes with such strength and power that the kids would look around to see what was happening. I can still see her black hair in my mind's eye with her choir robe on.

My mom and dad took us all to most every church dinner on Wednesday night. We knew that we were going to get something good when we went to the church for dinner – especially dessert. Plus, the program in the evening was always fun and involved getting up on the stage in Fellowship Hall.

We are huge Living Nativity fans too. As a child, it was special to dress up and be part of the program. I was mostly a shepherd. My sister Marguerite was an angel one year. My brother Patrick was a king. Hot chocolate and cookies were always provided by the church – even when it was 80 degrees out. I have fond memories of being a Shepherd with my church friend, Katie Ward.

I made new friends outside the school zone of my elementary and middle schools. Looking back, this was actually good because when I moved on from elementary, I knew some kids from church from other schools. It was nice to have my church friends from other elementary schools and middle schools.

Vacation Bible School was always a hit when I was younger. I remember going on the church bus to various outings in connection with VBS. I wanted every week to be a VBS week when I was growing up.

We also went to Youth Fellowship on Sunday evenings when the church had that activity. I think it was for 9th–12th graders. I remember being at church and walking out because it was snowing in Florida and we wrote on car windshields in the parking lot in the snow. It was around 1979.

One of my more interesting memories is when my parents made me go on a church retreat with the youth groups – a Friday and Saturday night. I really did not want to go, but they insisted. Other youth groups from other churches were there. It was when Ken Shick was the youth leader. When I came back home, my mother asked how it was and I told her that someone from another church group had offered me pot for the first time. Boy oh boy, she could not wait to tell Ken Shick about *that*!

I am grateful to have had a church home while growing up that fostered my Christian beliefs and helped shape my character in a fun and educational setting. Thank you to all present and past WPPC members, volunteers, and leaders.

Our Memories of WPPC

by Don and Sherri Erwin

Year 1980 was sort of special for Don and Sherri and their families. After earning his Master's degree in Civil Engineering from the University of Florida a year earlier, the Tallahassee firm where Don worked fell on hard times and had to downsize, leaving him looking for a new place to work and live. Having grown up in Tampa, he wanted to try a new place to live and accepted a job offer in Orlando.

Don's father had just retired as a minister at the Palma Ceia Presbyterian Church in Tampa after serving as a Team Minister for more than twenty years. His family had a small cottage at Montreat, North Carolina, and his parents had planned to continue service to the church by spending the winters in Tampa, where his dad would do interim pastorates, and the summers at the cottage. They had followed this routine for four years.

In 1982, after a couple of years at First Presbyterian Church downtown, Don decided to visit WPPC. It was smaller but of a similar size to the church in which he had grown up in Tampa. At the time Dr. Oswald Delgado, who was a seminary classmate of Don's father, was Senior Pastor. Reverend Glenn Bass and Dr. Ken Shick were Associate Pastors, and Dr. Bruce Cumming (retired) was a Parish Associate for visitation.

Don remembers Dr. Cumming coming to his apartment over on Semoran Blvd to visit him after his first visit to the church – what a wonderful person and pastor he was. Dr. Cumming provided him a warm, personal welcome and introduction to WPPC, and he decided this was the place for him.

Don soon became involved in the young adult program, choir, ushering, and other ministry activities. In the young adult group under the leadership of Reverend Ken Shick, he got to know Larry Seel, Mary Ham (Widick), Eric Boelzner, Mark Hecht, Caroline Berry, and others. Then Dr. Delgado announced his retirement after a long fruitful tenure as Senior Pastor, and the process to call a new pastor began. Dr. Cumming also retired (again); Dr. Bass and Dr.Shick were called to churches in Tallahassee and Tampa, respectively.

After the interim ministry of Dr. John Calvin Reid, Dr. Sherwood Anderson was called as the next Senior Pastor. In 1984, while the search was on to fill the two vacant Associate Pastor positions, the Session wanted to bring in an interim Parish Associate to fill the visitation role of Dr. Cumming, and to also provide experienced support for Dr. Anderson during the transition period. Hearing that Don's father, Rev. Donald Erwin, Sr., was retired and doing interim and supply pastor work in the Tampa area, Don was approached by a member of the Session to explore whether his dad might be interested in coming to WPPC temporarily until new, permanent Associate Pastors could be called. Don told them it was all right with him, and he didn't mind them giving him a call. They did, and after a formal invitation, Don's dad and mom moved to Winter Park in 1984.

One Sunday morning in 1985, while doing his regular usher duties (and sort of minding his own business), he noticed a new visitor at the 11:00 service, and several weeks later she came back. He learned that her name was Sherri Porter and she was going to graduate school at Rollins College.

She was living in Winter Park with her grandmother, Marjorie Klettner, an Episcopalian. Sherri's family back home in Houston was Presbyterian, so Mrs. Klettner asked her good friend and bridge partner, Louise Stanley of WPPC, if Sherri could go with her to her Presbyterian church.

Over a period of time Sherri became a regular visitor and joined the young adult group, where she and Don got to know each other better. The group grew over the next several months with young people from several churches including Ken Spirduso, Bethanne Seel, Glenn Widick, Doug Lovelace, and Jeanne Ackerman. It was a good group that did a lot of things together.

After about a year of just being friends, on July 31, 1986, Don and Sherri finally went on a "real" date, ending up at a square dance at WPPC, then going out afterwards. Don knew pretty soon that she was The One, and in October she said "yes." On April 11, 1986, Sherri and Don were married at WPPC because most of their friends and much of their family lived nearby. Don's dad performed the ceremony and Sherri's dad, a Presbyterian Elder, participated in the ceremony.

This is mentioned partly because of one unique thing about the wedding. Don and Sherri wanted to celebrate the sacrament of Holy Communion as part of the service (at a Presbyterian wedding? really?) and that is rarely done. Many had never heard of it. But of course they had to check the Book of Order to see if Presbyterians could really have Holy Communion at a wedding.

They found that it would be permitted, *but* in the Presbyterian Church, when Holy Communion is served, it must be offered to *all* who attend– the entire congregation (just like at regular worship). They didn't mind at all but did not anticipate the logistics that would be required, and didn't expect that the wedding would involve a full complement of communion servers. They included Dan Brown, George and Ginny Seel, Len and Mary Klusman, Mike and Vee Zimmerman, Hank and Glenda Lowrey, Flora Russell, Crawford and Marion Freeman, Norlin and Myrna Ham, Sue Rudolph, Corrine Dodd, Dora Hunter, and Al Porter (Sherri's dad). Fortunately, it worked out very well and it is still a great memory.

Time marches on and they soon were able to buy a home in Winter Park. They have raised two children, Rebekah and Andrew, in Winter Park. Both attended Sunday School and Youth Fellowship at WPPC. Both began at the WPPC Weekday Preschool under Mrs. Bensinger, which prepared them well to move on to Brookshire, Glenridge, and Winter Park High schools.

Sherri and Don have served as Elders and Deacons as well as adult and youth leaders. Daughter Rebekah served on the Presbytery Youth Council (PYC) and son Andrew earned his Eagle Scout rank in Troop 64, while Don and Sherri were adult leaders of the troop.

Both children have served as summer staff at the Montreat Conference Center Club Program for youth and children.

Winter Park Presbyterian Church is a large part of the history of our family: God's leading some family members to the church; another circumstance leading to the call of more family members to the church; a church member's invitation to a young adult to come to the church; two people meeting and developing a lasting relationship through the ministry to young adults; WPPC's ministry to little children, school children, older children, and adults. It's a great ministry to all – then, now, and in the future.

Youth Fellowship – and More

by Rosemary Magee

When Molly Magee was asked for her memories, she passed the query on to daughter Rosey (now Vice President at Emory University), who was 11 years old when the family came to WPPC. She and Elena Delgado were very close friends.

One memory is how impressed you and Dad were when we first moved to Winter Park and we visited various churches. We attended WPPC on Youth Sunday. Members of the youth fellowship contributed to the service in various ways: reading scripture, offering prayers, ushering, and the like. This really impressed you, and it was in part on that basis that you decided to join this church. You were also very impressed with the music program.

The church used to have a ministry in Zellwood with the migrant farmers. The youth fellowship was involved, and I remember one Saturday, Dad insisted on going with me (major embarrassment for me as a teenager) because he wanted to contribute as well.

You were recognized a number of years ago as an important contributor to the women in the church. And of course we all looked forward to Dr. Delgado's annual sermon, "Come Before Winter."

The Living Nativity Scene was also an annual event in our lives – that got complicated when a young male teenager insisted on being an angel, a roll traditionally assigned to girls at that time.

And then there was the night that the donkeys ran away!

Seems that there was never a dull moment!

Middle School Sunday School

by Donna Ettinger

In the early 2000s, the walls of the Middle School classroom had been painted a deep blue. Someone had painted cartoon characters on them. Garfield held court in one corner and Snoopy and Charlie Brown dominated another. I think Lucy was there, too.

One year, Dennis Lawson and I were teaching in that room and our students wanted to know if they could redecorate a bit. We agreed and they set to work. We found stickers along with crepe paper of various colors cut in strips, which we used. We spent one classperiod "decorating." By the time we finished, we had streamers hanging from every ceiling tile. They were just long enough to brush the heads of the students as they walked into the room. They loved their artistic "do over."

It was left up for a few weeks, and then we tried to take it down. Most of it was easily removed, but there were some pieces that we were still trying to reach for months after!

I don't know if anyone else appreciated our work, but the kids surely did.

The Advantages of Youth Fellowship

by Cathy Irwin Glinski

I met my husband at Winter Park Presbyterian Church Youth Fellowship in 1979. He was stationed at the Nuclear Power Training School in Orlando, and he was looking for a church. A friend brought him to the youth fellowship meeting one Sunday night, and we met. We started talking over volleyball and dinner, and five years later we were married at WPPC.

Twenty-nine years later, we are still very thankful for that youth fellowship meeting.

CHURCH LIFE ACTIVITIES

Wednesday Night and Other Dinners

by Ginny Seel

Once a month on a Wednesday night, we had a family night supper. Of course, because the congregation was so large at that time, we actually had two dinners each month. The congregation was divided into two parts alphabetically and then switched around the next month.

These were fun and delicious affairs. Our cook at the time was Bud Singleton and he knew what the congregation liked to eat – and eat we did.

There was always entertainment of some kind at these dinners. At times it came from within the membership and at other times by outside performers or some kind of lecturer or speaker.

The Family Life Committee was started around the 1970s and they also planned special dinners, usually on a Friday or Saturday night. There was a series of themed dinners that included a Mexican menu (with Mexican guitar players present), a Mardi Gras dinner, and one special Greek dinner. One of our members was a gourmet chef. He taught the women on the committee to make the main Greek entrée, with baklava for dessert. We learned a great deal and had so much fun and fellowship while learning.

Other activities included a square dance, talent shows, and performances by the teenagers and the choir.

It was truly a joy to be in this community of faith, which served not only those in need but also supported the friendships and fellowships within the congregation itself.

Christmas Caroling with the Chapel Choir

by Dana Irwin

One December afternoon in the mid-1990s, the Chapel Choir (children's choir) went Christmas caroling to some church shut-ins. We were in the church van, and they were wearing their bright blue choir robes. We stopped for the light at Lakemont and Aloma and a car pulled up beside us. The driver saw the children, and gave them applause and a thumbs-up.

That occupant was none other than Shaquille O'Neill! The children were beside themselves, needless to say. Their director got a boost as well.

How Often Do Your Grandchildren Surprise You?

by Carolyn and Glenn Collett
very proud grandparents

In May of 2012, I told our daughter, Michelle Trahan (an elementary school teacher) who teaches every summer at WPPC Vacation Bible School, that I would be happy to help; she would be teaching Arts and Crafts.

Then I told our granddaughters, Catherina and Jennifer Fields, that I would be working VBS as an assistant to their mom. Immediately, they started jumping up and down and screaming, "Yes, yes! Great, Nana!" I swelled with pride, thinking, "They really want me there!"

A bit later, their cousins Jarrett, Christina, and Shane Roberts (our daughter Kimberly Roberts' children) came over. Cat and Jen ran to them saying "Guess what? Nana will be working at VBS and our mom will be her *boss*. And get to tell Nana what to do!"(More jumping and screaming from all five.)

It wasn't what I expected all the excitement was about – but Nana and PopPop had to laugh.

Tea and Fashion Show

by Jeanne Vinci

I was a member of the Church Life Committee in the late '80s and can remember marveling at the brainstorming that would take place in committee, as we would plan suppers and somehow come up with an engaging theme or form of entertainment that would appeal to families and seniors alike. Granted, planning and implementing fellowship opportunities geared to strengthen our WPPC family bonds continues as a cornerstone of the Church Life Committee; however, decades ago the suppers were monthly events.

Thus, as we would seek God's intercession as we commenced meetings, we truly were calling out for him to help us at every level in the process! We would adjourn in faith that each of us would be able to deliver on the tasks assigned in time for the event.

There were culinary glitches and reservation issues and even steam issues when we decided to model environmental consciousness by nixing paper and plastic in favor of china and stainless! Of course, the repast was secondary to the richness of the experience as each occasion unfolded with warm camaraderie.

One such event was the Mother/Daughter Tea and Fashion Show that would be held the day before Mothers' Day. Di Schaefer was our connection with retail, and she handled the logistics of the show from outfit selections to transport, setting up of racks of clothes and accessories with diplomacy (think *"Does this dress make me look fat?"*) and aplomb!

The silver would be polished, the flowers arranged, and the buffet tables laden with trays of tiny sandwiches and colorful sweets. Lelah Edgell would set the tone for the main event by playing springtime tunes on the piano as mothers and daughters of every age would parade into the garden where yet another huge gathering of mothers and daughters would respond with affirming applause.

As the mother of daughters who now reside far from the beauty of this WPPC campus, the echoes of those golden celebrations of love for one another still warm my heart as I make my way along the covered walks each spring.

GROUPS

Women of the Church

from the Archives

The Women of the Church have always played a tremendous part in contributing to the work and outreach of this church.

One of the places where the phrase, "times have changed," is very evident is in the activities of the church today. If we would look to the history of Winter Park Presbyterian, we would find that back in 1953 one of the first groups in the church organization was the Women of the Church. Twenty-one women met to make these plans. It became a large and active organization, with many meetings and many smaller groups called Circles. The Circles usually met in the homes of the members. Women in those days were primarily homemakers and could adjust their schedules to include a morning or afternoon meeting.

To use their time productively as well as socially, the Winter Park Presbyterian Women met on other occasions to assist many church groups in different ways. Some would sew, others knit or crochet. This group made clothes for Thornwell and Duvall Home, refreshed clothes for missionaries returning home on furlough, Church World Service, Needlework Guild, and Sunland Hospital. The group grew to more than sixty women.

As our nation began to get back to normal after years of war, women had been spending their time attending college and getting advanced degrees. The workforce had changed. Women had replaced men who had been in the Armed Forces. Girls were graduating with degrees that were needed in business. The women, who had been homemakers in the past, were still homemakers, but a new method in homemaking had taken place. New products had hit the market that made housekeeping simpler. New entertainment inventions made it simpler to care for children. New businesses that provided professional child care enabled mothers to be away from home during the day.

The Women of the Church changed with the times to provide for meetings at night. The General Meeting of the Women had some of its meetings at night to include the Circles that could not be at a daytime meeting. These meetings often excluded older women who could not come to night meetings. This became the beginning of a decline in attendance. The women whose residences were at the two retirement homes in our area began meeting as Circles at their separate residences.

Securing leaders to guide this organization became difficult. The solution for the problem was to officially conclude the participation in this national organization in 2010. Three Circles still operate independently. One Circle continues to meet monthly in the evening at the church, one still meets at the church once a month in the morning, and another meets at Winter Park Towers once a month. Each Circle selects its own study. In the previous organization, a study was suggested and provided by the Department on Women's Work for the PC(USA). Where each Circle in the past collected an offering each month, and used a Blessing Box to decide what local project each circle would choose each year, the present Circles are primarily Bible-study groups, but they pray and show concern for the sick and needy.

Yes, times have changed, so let us look at the women at WPPC now. They are actively working in the church. They are members of the Session, the Deacons, the Choir, the Health Council, all of the church committees, the Sunday School, the Youth Groups, the IHS (feeding more than 200 at the Coalition for the Homeless), and the Health Council, and they volunteer every day as assistants in the Office, the Library, and the Friendship Club.

When women become ready to regroup and find a way that they can support a separate group for study, service, and fellowship, it will be time to rejoin the national church organization of Presbyterian Women. Until then, while we do not have an official organization of Presbyterian Women, we do have a multitude of Presbyterian Women in every phase of the life of the Winter Park Presbyterian Church.

Scouting at WPPC

from the Archives

The Scouting Program has been a part of WPPC since 1958, through the efforts of the Men of the Church and by the urging of Vernon Derr, who later became our first Scout Master. The Session sponsored the troop, which became Scout Troop #64 in October 1958.

In 1962, the Cub Pack with 150 boys was divided into two Packs. In September 1965, a new Cub Pack was organized by Tom Whitmore and William Ivey, son of the Reese Iveys, and was the first church-sponsored Boy Scout to receive the coveted God and Country award.

In 1964, the Explorer Post for 14- and 15-year-old boys was sponsored by the church, with Vernon Derr and Harry D. Warren Jr. as leaders.

In 1969, the Girl Scout Troop was approved and Cadet Troop #501 was established with Mrs. Robert (Jo) Stone as leader.

Many awards have been given to members of these scout troops including Eagle Scout, Star Scout, and God and Country, and Troup #64 continues to flourish.

WPPC and Troop 64

by Glenn Riccio

Winter Park Presbyterian Church has a distinguished 55-year history of involvement with the Boy Scouts of America through the sponsorship of Troop 64 Scout Troop and Cub Pack.

Since 1958, WPPC has provided a home for Troop 64 by giving the Scouts meeting space and allowing them to place a shed on the property for storing camping and Scouting supplies. In return, Troop 64 has provided support and mentoring for our boys and young men.

Troop 64 also helps with tasks around the church grounds, such as clearing the pre-school building roofs each year and gathering the pine needles necessary for setting up the Living Nativity event. WPPC has also benefitted from numerous Eagle Scout projects, resulting in improved landscaping and seating areas and some interior upgrades.

Over the past ten years, Troop 64 has been responsible for the advancement of sixteen Scouts to the rank of Eagle Scout, the highest rank offered by the Boy Scouts of America, for a total of fifty-nine Troop 64 Eagle Scouts since 1958.

Troop 64 is still very active. They have added a Venture Crew to the Cub and Scout program for youth who are too old to continue with the younger Scouts. Venture Crew allows young men and women up to the age of 21 to continue to be involved with scouting.

Among the three branches of BSA that are affiliated with WPPC, activities and events are always in progress, including monthly campouts to learn survival skills and summer camp, as well as family and special events that build teamwork and moral character with Troop members.

Session Experience

by Richard V. Sturm

Before Dr. Cuthill's arrival and during the time Dr. Anderson was here, I remember one Session meeting that started at the usual time of 7:30.

One of the Session members gave the opening devotional and it lasted a good twenty minutes with a long agenda still to go. The meeting ran on and on until about 10:45. Everyone was exhausted

The devotional person was quite put out that she didn't get to do the closing prayer, which she had prepared. It was a *long day*! Particularly when most of us had had a full day's work before we even arrived at this meeting.

End of Session work for me!

Presbyterian Women

by Corinne Jordan Dodd

The Presbyterian Women organization began many years ago when church women gathered to pray, study, and donate their money to help others. As women's roles have changed through the years, their contributions to the church have changed, but their dedication remains, and their leadership and work behind the scenes has influenced the entire membership and contributed hugely to the programs of each church.

The reunification of the church as the PC(USA) occurred in 1983, and in 1988 the Women of the Church was reorganized as Presbyterian Women. At Winter Park, the PW continued the tradition started in 1954 to choose women – and occasionally a man – to be honored with a Life Membership award. The selection was based on an individual's commitment to Christ and the mission of the church. These people were honored each year on "Celebrate the Gifts of Women Sunday," and were presented with a certificate and symbolic pin.

Each name on the following list reflects a life that is dedicated to faithful service. This list ends in 2009 at the dissolution of the Presbyterian Women. As most women either work outside the home or are active as Deacons and Elders, leadership within the organization became difficult to sustain and it was reluctantly dissolved.

Honorary Life Members

1954 Dr. Freemont Vale
1955 Kathryn Fosgate
1957 Imogene Johnston
1958 Sally McDowall
1959 Helen Rice
1960 Betty Whittaker
1961 W. Cecil Sewell
1961 Mrs. G. Comstock
1961 Theresa Scott
1962 Elizabeth Rice
1962 Charles E. Potter
1962 Barbara Potter
1962 William Caldwell
1963 Katherine Faucett
1964 Delia Delgado
1964 Anne Lawton
1965 Catherine Badger
1965 Helen Smith
    (First Pres Miami)
1966 Mary Nusbickel
1966 Jean Warren
1967 Mary Derr
1967 Ruth Smith
1967 Mrs. Walter Hewitt
1968 Linda Erd
1969 Shirley Call
1969 Maggie Ivey
1969 Jo Stone
1969 Dr. Oswald
    Delgado
1969 Peg Anderson
    (First Pres Hollywood)
1970 Ann Divine
1970 Ori Sue Jordan
1971 Freda Regan
1971 Dot Robinson
1972 Marlin Pankey
1972 Dot Steele
1972 Walter N. Hewitt
1973 Louise Guthrie
1973 Lou Hollingshead
1974 Phylis Cramer
1974 Ruby Matthews
1974 Ruth Wainwrght
1975 Clara Adolfs
1976 Bea Langford

1976 Marguerite
    Richards
1976 Hope Larsen
1976 Mildred Morgan
1977 Eva Bele
1977 Lillian Urschel
1978 Ruth Parrish
1978 Marian Pyle
1979 Dot Campbell
1979 Dr. Bruce
    Cumming
1979 Marian Fleming
1979 Althea Keim
    (John Knox, Orlando)
1980 Verna Lynch
1980 Dorothy Storms
1980 Carol Woolley
1981 Robert Stone
1981 Mrs. Kenneth
    Thomas
1982 Elizabeth
    Brownlee
1982 Ann Butler
1982 Gladys Jellison
1982 Ruthie Schreiber
1983 Joan Newman
1983 Gerry Elliis
1983 Mary Steele
    Cooper
1984 Melody Barrett
    (First Pres Delhi, NY)
1984 Jean Kouba
1985 Genevieve Lewis
1985 Dot Carlie
1986 Ruth Thompson
1986 Patricia
    Williamson
1987 Martha Gould
1987 Mary Ellen
    Priester
1988 Lucy Aldrich
1989 Mabel Deaney
1990 Corinne Jordan
    Dodd
1990 Mary Virginia
    Lawrence

1991 Ida Edwards
1991 Louise Reid
1992 Virginia Lockman
1992 Robert Shrigley
1993 Ginny Seel
1994 Sally Blake
1995 Richard Fuquay
1995 Catherine Hudson
1995 Rose Walters
1996 Carrie Hollman
1996 Bonnie Wilhite
1998 Myrna Erwin
1998 Louise Stanley
1998 Richard Sturm
1999 Mildred Baggett
1999 Faye Klang
1999 Sue Rudolph
2000 Sallie Mikesell
    Hadley
2000 Jean Carolan
2000 Molly Magee
2001 Audrey Gantt
2001 Dee Herschel
2001 Betty Hines
2001 Mary Danielson
    (Boynton Beach)
2002 Dora Hunter
2003 Betty Gow
2003 Xandra Roth
2003 Bobbi Jo Walker
2004 Phyllis Woods
2004 Mary Klusman
2004 Rene Cuthill
2005 Mary Beardall
2005 Mary Naughtin
2006 Martha Campbell
2006 Julia Rankin
2007 Barbara Edwards
2007 Jean Ross
2007 Sadie Singleton
2008 Cora Evans
2008 Anne Murray
2009 Marilyn Bryant
2009 Rev. George
    Campbell

So Many Memories

by Miriam Sprague

I am not a writer but I have fond memories that I know many others must share. Who could forget the Friendship Club, a source of real friendships, not to mention the delicious lunches and wonderful programs?

And I have enjoyed many wonderful years in the choir and as a bell ringer. These are more than musical groups. They are families.

Our church has the benefit of an extra dimension with the trips abroad, led so many times by Dr. Cuthill. I especially enjoyed the trip to the Holy Land. There is an old hymn, *I Walked Today Where Jesus Walked*, and I truly felt that I had walked in His footsteps.

What a joy it has been to share.

WHIP

by Bob Miller

In the late 1960s in the Theresa Scott Sunday School class, a group of WP Presbyterian members formed an investment club called WHIP: **We Hope Investment Pays.**

The club meets monthly for lunch and has a party with wives once a year. The club has been in continual operation since its founding.

Listed here are WHIP members who are or were members of WP Presbyterian Church.

Jack Aebli (investment adviser)	Roland Lee
Cliff Canada	Bob Miller
Bob Cramer	Steve Miller
Dave Collier	George Seel
Herb Hazzard	Harry Warren
Chappy Lawton	

I believe all original WHIP members were either Deacons or Elders and WWII veterans. One of the originals is still a member – Roland Lee. However, Roland left Winter Park in the 1960s to help start the Tuskawilla Presbyterian Church, where he is still active.

Friendship Club

by Martha Campbell

The American Heritage Dictionary defines "club" as "a group of people organized for a common purpose, especially a group that meets regularly."

The Friendship Club, formerly the 60-PLUS Fellowship, was organized in 1978 and had its first meeting in November. It was formed to meet the need for Christian fellowship among the senior members of the Church, friends, and guests by having luncheons and monthly trips (originally called safaris) to interesting places. The Club name change was made in 1992 in order to include many members and guests who had *not* reached 60 years of age. That also made us consistent with other similar church groups that have no age restrictions.

The Club year starts in September with a luncheon meeting and continues through the month of May with an occasional meeting in June. The meetings are held on the first Friday of each month, except on those months when a national or church holiday is close to that date. The Steering Committee arranges and schedules the monthly trips or activities, which are normally held on the third Friday of the month. You may look for program details in the Sunday *Bulletin*.

While we are known as a club, there are *no* dues. Luncheons and programs are moderately priced, and the trip costs vary depending on the destination and the fees charged, if any. Reservations are necessary.

The Friendship Club has *no* membership rolls; however, we do have a telephone listing of active participants. Anyone wishing to be on this list in order to be notified of the meetings or special events can be added to this list by calling the church office at (407) 647-1467.

About fourteen years ago, the Club organized a food-product-of-the-month project to assist local food banks. Each month the Club is asked to donate a designated nonperishable food product. We are currently donating our products to the Winter Park Family Emergency Services.

So we have a club that has no dues and no membership rolls, but it meets regularly for good food, good fellowship, and great friends. Won't you join us at 11:30 a.m. on first Fridays in Fellowship Hall? All are welcome, and we look forward to meeting and greeting you.

KumBaya

by Pat Brown

One program that our church initiated in the 1990s is no longer functioning, but it served a great purpose at the time.

KumBaya was a program designed to give neighborhood kids a place to go after school. It was inaugurated in 1979 and was successful, but very expensive to maintain. When the local YWCA began a similar program toward the end of that same year, ours became redundant and was discontinued. It is noted, though, that the church saw a need and filled it – and did so before the Y stepped in and took it over.

SPECIAL PROJECTS

Early Cyber Days at WPPC

from the Archives

When computers were a novelty and many people had been using them for several years, a minister from Ohio started preparing materials to be used with computers to teach children in the Sunday School. WPPC sent a group of leaders and youth to Atlanta to learn how this method could be used. This group came back full of enthusiasm and made plans to ask members of the congregation to give their old computers to the church so they could be reconditioned for use in a Computer Center at the church.

In 1998, the Computer Center became a reality. Jodi Parker, an engineer at Lockheed-Martin, and her husband, Todd Parker, both WPPC members and Youth Sunday School teachers, began purchasing the necessary parts for the Computer Renewal. They were joined by other WPPC members, Doug Reece, and a number of computer literate youth, who spent many sessions outfitting the computers with necessary replacements and software.

Mark Wilson, a WPPC member electrician, gave of his time to do all the necessary reworking of the wiring, thus providing the necessary electricity and Internet and printer accessibility for six computers.

Bill Smith, a retired WPPC churchman, gave his time to plan and construct four standing screens to separate the computer units.

In 1999, the Media Center Room included the Computer Center with six individual stalls. Each stall contained a computer table, computer, monitor, keyboard, and two speakers. Each computer had access to one basic printer.

Soon after the opening of the Computer Center, classes for Basic Computer were taught by some WPPC professionals. Among them were the Reverend Jim Tinkey and Dr. Lynn Hartle for adults, and several Weekday Preschool class teachers for the children.

Since content for the teaching for children was provided by DVDs, it proved to be very expensive to buy a separate DVD for each computer. And it was illegal to make copies for each computer from one DVD. The cyber age was beginning to advance rapidly. The Internet was becoming vital to everyone with a computer. It offered many free programs for children as well as adults.

The Weekday Preschool suggested that the old computers be replaced with newer ones that could provide free teaching material for use with the Preschool students. New computers were secured and for years, the church provided a computer room for teaching children and adults.

Time marches on and now the computer has become a part of most homes and the school has moved on from this part of their curriculum. The church continues to use the advanced developments of the cyber age. The Church web site is an important part of the church's program. Announcements are sent to the congregation through the web site. The Covenanter is produced and sent to the congregation through the web site. The Library is providing the listing of the Library books on the web site.

We do not know what will be the next development for the church to include in its teaching program, but I am sure that it will stay abreast of the times in which we live and there will be those in this great congregation that can provide the essential skills to teach the churches' message in whatever ways it must use.

Introducing Computers

by Ginny Seel

In 1982 and 1983, I was working at the church as a Church Life secretary while my husband was out of the country for an extended period of time.

The Chair of the Personnel Committee approached me with the following information – and a question for me.

The church was getting ready to purchase our very first computers and it needed someone who was familiar with the membership to do data entry. I agreed and spent many hours typing in names, addresses, and all that. And I finally completed the current membership information.

One of our Associate Ministers was fascinated with the computer. One morning when I came in, I found that everything I had entered up to that time had been erased! The minister in question had been there the night before trying to become familiar with it and had inadvertently deleted all that I had entered!

I was frustrated, of course, but he was so apologetic that I felt badly for him, and I began all over. Did it all again.

Andy Manking and Bill Branch were a great help to us in getting the system going and training us to use the software. Now look where we are – thirty years later.

The Stephen Ministry

by Gigi Erwin, R.N., FCN

In the summer of 2011 the Health Cabinet and I talked about the possibility of starting a Stephen Ministry. A Stephen Ministry consists of laypeople who receive fifty hours of training to provide caring support to those who are going through a difficult time. Some people thought we would not have anyone who would be willing to go through those fifty hours and then commit to two years of service. I decided to do a church-wide survey to learn how much interest people had. Amazingly, we found seven people with interest in becoming a Stephen Minister.

The first training class started in January 2012 and five people attended the training sessions every Tuesday night for five months. They learned how to really listen, and how to walk beside someone who is experiencing a loss. Stephen Ministers provide care to people who are going through a difficult time. They may have lost a loved one or have a terminal illness.

Or perhaps they are separated or divorcing, or are experiencing job loss; they might be relocating, or be chronically ill or disabled; others may be military spouses, or caretakers of ill or disabled persons.

The best way to describe what Stephen Ministers do is to say that they care; they "bear one another's burdens, and in this way...fulfill the law of Christ."

Stephen Ministers usually meet with their care receivers once a week for about an hour and may also talk with them over the phone, depending on the needs of the situation. Stephen Ministers listen, care, pray, support, and encourage in an environment of complete confidentiality.

I attended sixty hours of Stephen Ministry Leadership Training in June 2012 and in July, after a commissioning service, a new ministry was born at WPPC!

We have five Stephen Ministers – each is assigned to a care receiver, working behind the scenes to provide support. They are Dawn Sumrall, Jayne Leach, Jeanne Vinci, Ellenorr Osterhaus, and Patrick Mullen.

Now, in May 2013, we have two additional Stephen Ministers who have just completed their training and will be commissioned in June – Carol Howell and Curtis Harrison.

God has richly blessed this ministry as is evidenced in our monthly meetings (please note that names are never mentioned to protect confidentiality), and we look forward to seeing what God will do through this Ministry as the future unfolds.

Walk to Bethlehem

by Dawn Sumrall

My first experience as a member of the Health Cabinet in 2012 was to volunteer to make the map for the Walk to Bethlehem. Our church had never tried walking and tallying our miles, then submitting them weekly, to see if we could Walk to Bethlehem during the Advent season.

Each week, our Parish Nurse told me how far the participants at WPPC had walked and I would advance the markers on the map, along with arrows, to show the members of our congregation how we were doing.

It was so joyous to see how, individually and collectively, we joined in walking each day – and reached our goal well before Christmas.

Good health habits were created, and also our Interim Minister, Pastor Tim Rogers-Martin, was able to use this Walk to Bethlehem theme for his Advent sermons. A win-win circumstance all around.

Screen-Door Visit Program

by Betty Gow

Sometime around 1995, a member of the Evangelism Committee (that name has been changed several times over the years) started to develop a program for first-time visitors to the church. Before she was able to accomplish this, she had to leave Winter Park for health reasons and asked me to take over until her return. However, she never returned!

With a lot of help from many volunteers, a successful program was developed. Anna Johnston and I baked "Bread Wreaths" from frozen yeast rolls, and I packaged them. They were accompanied by a brochure about the church history and activities, and were tied with a scotch-plaid ribbon. We wrote a personal note inviting the visitor to church.

Any visitor who gave us an address was visited and handed the package at the door (if they were at home). If they were not home, we left the package at the front door so they would find it when they returned.

The program was a success until technology and a "cultural change" brought it to a stop. With the increased use of computers, e-mail addresses started taking the place of street addresses. As families became busier, they no longer wanted to take the time for yeast rolls to rise and bake. So grocery stores stopped carrying frozen yeast rolls in favor of already baked rolls.

Barbara Edwards worked very hard to carry on the program, but eventually she found that she had to give it up.

The Great Quilt

by Jeanne Vinci

"The Kingdom of God is as if a woman should gather bits and pieces of cloth, taking the best of each, for a great quilt... As she stitches the pieces together, the narrative is formed. It is a story of joy and survival, compassion and laughter. It is an expression of her feelings about her life before and her life to come, her past and her destiny, her memories and her hopes..." Dr. Robert D. Gamble

Thus began Dr. Gamble's sermon based upon parables Jesus shared, "using the stuff of his day" in order to connect with the listeners gathered round him. The sermon progressed comparing the "bits and pieces" that made up the inspiring narrative of Jesus' ministry to the scores of seemingly unrelated "bits and pieces" that contributed to the sum total of each day in the life of this young minister, to the hundreds of "bits and pieces" that combined to continuously support the dynamic mission of Winter Park Presbyterian Church.

He also pointed to the challenges posed when purposefully planned schedules, designed to foster a smooth path to achieving goals, would be interrupted time and again by the errant "bits and pieces" of life!

In summation, Robert Gamble recognized that there is a measure of grace to the process of ministry as well as life. "In spite of our planning, in spite of all our programs, in spite of all we do or fail to do...because it doesn't always go right, it doesn't always go the way we want it to, it doesn't always make sense, in the church or in our lives... In spite of this, something beautiful will emerge..."

Indeed, something beautiful, something most precious had recently emerged, pinned to a clothesline in the center of the stage in Fellowship Hall during a potluck supper on the evening of June 12, 1991 – the very quilt that inspired the sermon. Dana Irwin and Margie Meliza, two of the busiest members of the WPPC church family, launched the friendship quilt project as a tangible farewell for our family.

The congregation at the time was involved in a major renovation, sowing seeds for a pipe organ campaign and a pastoral search committee was in the process of forming; a progressive and at times hectic climate similar to that which presents as we celebrate our sixtieth year as a family of Christ.

Defying logic, a group of stalwarts who were already stretched to their limits in service felt called to organize in still another loving outreach project! Margie designed the scheme and kits were assembled with the essential coordinated materials so that each family could personalize designs for their particular squares.

In addition, each contributor was asked to document the significance of the special memory symbolized in the square for collection in "The Vinci Family Friendship Album Quilt" notebook.

Names neatly placed in numbered squares on graph paper include Lynn Bernstein, Jeanne Cook and family, the Don Erwin family, the Felkel family, Beth Girard, Dana Irwin, the Iselin family, Margie Meliza and family, Ellenorr Osterhaus and family, Sue Rudolph, Brenda Stutler, Ruth Thompson, and Bonnie Wilhite. Bonnie and Margie pinned the top for Dana's expert hands to sew. Betty Lee joined Barbara, Ruth, Dana, Bonnie, Jeanne, and Jennifer Cook for yet another full day of tying with Don and Sherri Erwin smoothing the material.

Snapshots taken during the process reflect a grueling task accomplished in the heat of summer by gracious individuals who clearly recognized the pure joy that comes through commitment to others.

Clearly this band of servant-leaders inspired the congregation as the word slipped out about their considerable undertaking in the midst of challenge.

Families and staff filled twelve long tables during a potluck that was quietly organized for the unveiling and surprise dedication of the friendship quilt. Fellowship Hall was infused with jubilation as the success of the project was celebrated.

The affirmation of our own family equated to an affirmation of the greater WPPC family, as this outreach was illustrated so beautifully.

The WPPC Friendship Quilt remains the most treasured tangible in our household. We hand-carried the quilt in its special case during each and every one of our moves across this country. Guests would be drawn to the masterpiece on the wall and recognize that even though, as a military family our stay would be short, we might be worth a closer look because the Winter Park church family had clearly been dazzled by the Vincis!

As anyone that has moved can attest, the learning curve is steep and the just plain hard work involved in settling in to a home while making a life takes a certain amount of courage. The squares on the quilt would provide comfort during each transition, as we would share reflections about our years at Winter Park. Perhaps even more important, the investment of time, talent, labor, and love would provide the catalyst necessary to set each of us in our own way on the path of service to others in the unique situations – indeed breathtaking moments – that God provides time after time.

Bits and pieces of life…

TRAVEL AND OUTINGS

Memories of My Years at WPPC

by Sadie Singleton

As told to Richard Small on April 26, 2013 at Sunbelt Apopka Health and Rehab Center.

Before my husband James and I joined WPPC in 1989, I worked for several years in the day nursery. One day the pastor asked me if I was a member of another church. I answered, "Yes, New Hope Baptist Church." He then asked, "When do you go?" I said, "I don't." So he invited me to join WPPC. I had loved working for Mrs. Derry and I had loved the children I cared for there. It seems that they loved me, too, and Kathryn Fosgate had even said that I practically raised her twins. So we joined. I still love this church and its people so much.

One of my favorite WPPC memories is going to Israel with a group of other church members and led by Dr. Cuthill. I had not planned to go because I didn't have enough money, but when my children heard about it, they said, "You're going. We're paying. Call them right now and make your reservation." I have three wonderful children, Sadie Lou, James, and Larry (not to mention twenty-nine grandchildren and ten great grandchildren).

It was a wonderful trip, but there were moments of stress. Let me tell you about one of them. We had crossed the border into Jordan to tour there, and when we returned I was held back by a Jordanian border guard for a passport issue, and nobody in my group was aware of it! They got on the tour bus before realizing I wasn't with them! Fortunately, one of them spotted me. Dr. C came over to where I was and asked the border guard, "What's the problem?" He responded, "Her passport. This woman (pointing to me) isn't as old as the person in this passport. They are *not* the same person!" Dr. C said, "We haven't had a problem until now, and besides, I have known Sadie Singleton a long time. I'm her minister and I know her age. I want her released so we can continue with our trip." Finally the border guard let me go. Later, Larry said to me, "He was right, Sadie. You *don't* look your age." After that Larry told Rene Cuthill to keep an eye on me.

I learned a thing or two on that trip. I learned that the water in the Black Sea is as clear as tap water in a glass. Back home someone argued with me that it was not. Phyllis Woods overheard and intervened, telling the other woman that what I said was true.

We saw two unusual homes over there and I talked to the residents. One was a single-story house owned by a couple with two young sons. But it had pipes and things sticking up out of the roof. It looked unfinished. The owner told me that when their oldest son marries, he would build a second story and live there, and the next oldest son, when he marries, would build a third floor. "Why?" I asked. It was because of the shortage of real estate to build on.

In another town – Petra, I think – I observed a very poor family that lived near a body of water in a cave that had been hollowed out by the flow of storm water. It was below street level. They had to use donkey-driven carts to get from one level to the other. A little girl who lived there was selling pretty rocks to make some money. I bought some and the mother thanked me.

Now here's a funny story I'd like to tell about my children. It was a July Fourth. My husband James had to work that day at WPPC to help complete the installation of some new pews, including dusting and loading the pew racks with books and things, plus sweeping some walkways, and that sort of thing. The children, especially Sadie Lou, had hoped to go to the beach that day. But I insisted that all three of them must "help their daddy" so he could finish and get off early. Sadie Lou was very disappointed and said, "Okay, I'll do it, but I sure don't want to!"

Later, Dr. Delgado happened to walk by where Sadie Lou was working and she said, "Dr. Delgado, I want to speak to you. When I marry, and if you are still here, I want *you* to clean up afterwards. And we're not going to pay you one dime, because you made us work on the Fourth of July!" Dr. Delgado came inside where I was working and told me about the encounter and I thought he would never stop laughing. He said to me, "Sadie, that was a big order and I'm going to put that on my to-do list right now!"

I have been close to the people of WPPC since before I even joined. When James passed away, it became especially important to me. Because of health problems, I've been in a rehab facility recently. It's a good place, but it's not home and it's hard to go to church, though I sometimes get to. My health problems seem to be improving now, and at my last doctor's appointment, he said, "Sadie, everything checks out." So I am looking forward, with hope, to returning home and getting back to the church and the people that I love so much.

WPPC Goes To Montreat

from the Archives

Montreat Conferences, held on the campus of Montreat College in Montreat, North Carolina, have been on the WPPC agenda for many years. In the 1990s and 2000 two main groups found fun and inspiration at this beautiful mountain retreat that has been part of the Presbyterian Church since the late 1800s.

The Senior High Youths have had large groups attend the Youth Conferences. Since the year 2000, many of the Christian Educators, Youth Adult Advisors, and many other adults interested in the Youth Ministry have accompanied the youth to the General Assembly Youth Conferences.

Some of the past leaders such as Don and Sherri Erwin, Drew and Susie Marshall, and Mike and Dorothy Burk drove the bus, planned and cooked the meals, and supervised the house that was rented by the church and where the youth stayed for the week. Others served as Advisors and Counselors to the youth as they attended the conferences and participated in other activities such as recreation, athletics, art, or rock-hopping in Flat Creek.

The Older Adult Group (60+, later the Friendship Club) attended the Older Adult Conferences on several occasions. On one trip, I remember the group traveling in a caravan – three cars drove together, round-trip. They stayed in cottages owned by WPPC members and attended the conference and its activities held at the Montreat Conference Center Hotel at the Assembly Inn.

On other occasions, the group joined the First Presbyterian Church of St. Petersburg for the trip, going in a commercial tour bus. They stopped overnight in Savannah one way and had an evening on the waterfront during the return trip. This enabled those in the older group to have easy transportation, with housing and conference in one hotel.

Montreat is enjoyed by other members of WPPC as a retreat during the summer, with a Day Camp for children and golf for adults, hiking for the able, concerts and art for the arty, and a quiet mountain stream for reading and listening.

Field Trips

by Dana Irwin

The participants in the various music ministries have gone on several field trips through the years. The Chancel Choir, Youth Choir, Children's' Choir, and the Bell Choirs have performed at Winter Park Towers, the Naval Base Chapel, Manor Care, and other local venues.

The farthest traveled has been by those attending the Montreat Music Conference in North Carolina. From about 1978 to the present, there have been quite a few trips to that enriching conference by as many as twelve musicians and as few as one.

Once there, we are immersed in creative worship experiences, wonderful Bible studies, and singing and ringing choirs lead by outstanding, world-famous conductors. There is also time to relax and enjoy the lovely mountain setting.

Those attending have stayed in the college dorms, private homes, rental homes, and the local motel.

The handbell choirs traveled to Lakeland several times to participate in workshops conducted by renowned handbell composers/directors. As many as twenty-five choirs participated, so the bells really made joyful sounds. We also hosted such a workshop here at WPPC on one occasion.

During the 1990s, the children's choir participated in the Choristers' Guild Festival, going to different churches in the Central Florida area for a day of rehearsing music that had been selected in the fall for the festival. Each church used those anthems throughout the year, and then polished them with a nationally known conductor at the festival for the performance at the end of the day.

The children also had a chance to explore other ways to interpret music (handbells, Orff instruments, sign language, dance) as part of the activities.

All who participated in the many music field trips have, I am sure, a lot of pleasant memories of the travels, the music, and the new friends they found.

Memories of WPPC

by Meg and Rusty Baldwin

Among our fondest memories from our years at WPPC are the annual family campouts at Moss Park. Glenn Bass led the campouts in the mid-1970s and early 1980s. Many of the families would travel to Moss Park on a Friday afternoon after a stop at Popeye's for their famous Fried Chicken!

Campsites were set up, the kids would gather together and play while the grownups visited and prepared a pig to be roasted on the open fire pit. Saturday usually included some hiking and canoeing in the lake. A family soft ball game was traditional, and as the day ended, the famous Ar-Ar-Ar-Ar-ma-dilllll-aaaaa Hunt would begin! There was much calling and noise-making, trying to scare an "armadillo" out of the woods! The pig was finally roasted, dishes were brought out to share, and blessings were asked all around. Campfires, songs, stories, and s'mores ended the day!

In the quiet of Sunday morning, we would gather by the lake and sing "Morning Has Broken." Glenn would share his thoughts and we would pray together as families and friends.

How thankful we are for those memories and friends!

HURRICANES

After Hurricane Charley

by Myrna Erwin

There are many memories of Winter Park Presbyterian Church that I will never forget. However, I want to tell about one memory that exemplifies the heart of this church. It occurred in August 2004 when we were all facing the same trauma. After Hurricane Charley was past, I went to the church to see if the books in the Library had survived the storm. I do not think the office staff was there at that time because I heard a telephone that kept ringing and I answered it. A person who lived on a street behind the church wanted to know if she could run an extension cord to the church and get electrical power, because her house was without power. She needed power to prepare food for her family.

I told her I could not answer her question about the power, but if she would come to church, I would see if she could get some food collected by the church for a Food Pantry. She came and found a supply of food that could be served cold that would help feed her family. Her family also borrowed books from the Library to enable her six children to be entertained during this period of disaster. The church got power back quickly, because it is on the same grid as the hospital.

Later that day, some other people from the church came to check the kitchen at the church. They found that power for the freezer and refrigerator had been off during storm and it would be wise to cook the food that had not completely thawed before it would be lost. Someone suggested that we should prepare the food, and invite the people in the neighborhood around the church to come that evening for dinner.

The invitation was placed on the church sign facing Lakemont. That evening Fellowship Hall was full of folks from the neighborhood. It was an amazing crowd. Everyone pitched in to help serve. Whole families gathered at tables and church members went about serving and visiting with their neighbors. Also in attendance were some of the out-of-state power workers who had come to help Florida.

People who came to worship that first Sunday brought their cell phones with them to charge. Every outlet had a phone connected to it!

During the week following the storm, things began to settle down. It was time to check the church building for damage. The most evident was the cupola that had blown from the top of the bell tower over the church entrance. It did not hit anyone but fell onto the front lawn.

Many leaks were evident in the rooms, and the library books, though not damaged by water, required individual wiping to remove the dust and dampness. The Youth Group came to the rescue. They worked long hours to wipe each individual book with dry towels and wiped shelves with disinfectant to be sure the vast collection of valuable books was saved. Since half of the books in the Library are next to windows, the church staff had put large sheets of plastic on the windowed wall to keep the rain out. That plastic is still in place, awaiting another hurricane that may come in the future.

This whole experience brought the church together is a way that was special. We all were in the same situation. All were affected by a terrible storm. All saw the needs of the community. Out of the community's need came thoughts of helping others that had problems that needed to be solved. The church ministered to the community, and became the beacon that was its real purpose. Even though its cupola was lying damaged in the grass.

Hurricane Charley – Summer of 2004

by Jill Poole

Our church was without power for days after Charley, so a decision was made to empty our freezers and cook all the perishable food for the neighborhood. It was a tremendous effort and people started arriving as soon as the doors opened.

Teams of cooks and other helpers worked nonstop and my job was to clear tables or check if anything was needed. I came to a family with two young boys and asked if they needed anything more. "No thank you," was the polite reply.

"How about another drink?"

"Another drink? Can we really?"

"Of course," I replied, "and how about some ice?"

Ice? Real ice? Their eyes opened wide. They could not believe it. Such a simple thing but they were still talking about it as they left for home.

I will never forget their faces and those of all the other visitors to WPPC that day, including the Fire Department, who had all been working so hard.

PERSONALITIES

Fifty-Five-Plus Years at WPPC

by Wyatt Gantt
as told to Richard Small

This interview was conducted April 9, 2013 at The Westchester. Sadly, Wyatt Gantt passed away just days later. His final service was held at WPPC on April 18, 2013.

I worked for Martin Marietta in Baltimore and moved to Orlando in 1957 to help start up the plant here. I was proud of my career. I liked working in propulsion. As a group engineer on one such project, I made a jet engine out of a B-29 impeller and a set of reaction vanes. About 1990, the Property Committee was confronted with the prospect of replacing all plumbing in the church building, which was copper piping. This was at a great cost if conventional galvanized piping were to be used.

Instead, a proposal to use a chemical technique called "electrolysis" was utilized, which saved thousands of dollars to repair the leaking piping. Several so-called engineers on the committee spoofed this approach, calling it fool's play (or black magic).

Hi-tech does have wonders today, doesn't it?

•*I remember* a problem we once had with the kitchen. Although Fellowship Hall was air-conditioned, the kitchen was not, and it was a sweat shop. Bud Singleton, the chef, had to work in there. It was very hot for him, but he never complained; he was a great guy. He had been a chef at the Angebilt Hotel until he arrived at WPPC to cook for us. Some members of the Property Committee believed that installing air-conditioning in the kitchen couldn't be done. But I was an engineer and I disagreed. I knew that with proper air handling and ducting, coupled with an exhaust hood over the ovens, it *could* be done. We called an A-C professional to design a system for us. Then Burt Woodruff hired a contractor to do the installation, and it worked well. I felt so good about the project that I contributed $1,000 toward it and others contributed as well. My wife said, "You gave *how* much?"

•*I remember* Bud's wife, Sadie Singleton, a faithful and cheerful person. Her daughter was a singer and once she brought in a choir of other young people and sang many of the Negro classics, such as spirituals. They raised the roof! It was quite a different experience for WPPC. Other youth choirs visited, some on tour from foreign countries, to perform for WPPC. We had good turnouts. Church members provided lodging for them at their homes. It was a great program.

•*I remember* taking WPPC youths to the migrant work camps in West Virginia nine times. We worked on tar roofs, added porches, and installed electrical service in the migrants' cabins. While working on an electric circuit in one cabin, we almost blew it up. One of the youths said, "I can do it," and threw the switch before it was ready. BOOM!

Each trip lasted two weeks. We'd take one or two vans and as many as twenty-five or thirty people, bringing our own tools but getting lumber locally. The kids would do all the work. Sometimes they'd get into "tar fights," with predictable results.

•*I remember* serving as an officer in WPPC over the span of thirty years, a Deacon three times, and an Elder three times. I was also a member of the church choir for two years. My wife Audrey was ill with cancer, and wanted me to join the choir. I thought I couldn't sing, but she taught me to sing the same notes as the guy next to me, and it worked! I was a novice at music, but I enjoyed it very much.

•*I remember* Eric Boelzner as a young man – now the son-in-law of Ken Shick.* Eric became an Elder at age 22. I sponsored him. Some people thought he was too young, but I knew differently. I have two daughters who were active in the youth program under Ken. At first they shied away because their dad was at the church. They felt like PKs (preachers' kids) and didn't want to feel tied down. Each daughter has a son and daughter of her own now. I keep my favorite picture of my family on the wall here at The Westchester, including my late wife Audrey, my daughters, their husbands, and their children.

•*I remember* WPPC as being one of the best churches in the area, with aggressive, successful programs and social activities. Our youth program was super under Ken Shick. Because of my experience at WPPC, I am more spiritual now. I have enjoyed visits from old and new WPPC friends.

Richard said, just before he terminated the interview, "I have one more question that I just have to ask: Are you the man who invented the Gantt Chart?" Smiling broadly, Wyatt responded, "That question haunted me all during my time at Martin Marietta. No, that was a different Gantt, though it was spelled the same."

* Ken Shick was an Associate Pastor and Youth Minister in the 1970s and '80s.

Memories

by Marilyn and Tom Simmons

Our fond memories go back to the 1980s and '90s when Winter Park enjoyed the interim ministry of Dr. Robert Gray. Dr. Gray was not only a person with a great pastoral message for all ages, but he was also noted for being a very personable minister in one-on-one exchanges with everyone he encountered.

He had served eighteen years as pastor at the Park Lake Church in Orlando before he took a sojourn to Lafayette, North Carolina, to be near his eldest daughter and husband. At the moment of retirement, he tragically lost his wife in an auto accident, just before they were to return to reside in Central Florida. He had this heavy grief to bear in those early days.

At the same time, Winter Park was in search of an interim pastor, having lost the previous minister in a contentious parting.

It was providential that both Winter Park and Dr. Gray, at this same time, had a lot of healing to do; he and our congregation served each other symbiotically in such a beautiful manner of restoration. Winter Park regained its historic mission in serving the community and congregation at a pivotal time in his ministry.

He was recognized as a true Scot, in that his mother was native to Scotland. He would perform in full Scotsman attire and regalia, with an accented monologue that was entertaining for us all. He initiated our popular Kirkin' of the Tartan worship service.

He now lives in full retirement in Atlanta. The Park Lake church, where he served for so many years, honored him by naming him Pastor Emeritus.

Lee Hall

by Matt Straub

I remember the first time I came to this church. Some of us were born and bred here, but the majority of us have walked through the door, tentatively, as first-timers – not sure what to expect – maybe even a little guarded.

I arrived on a grey, rainy January Sunday morning. People were friendly. What struck me most was the high glass wall at the rear of the Sanctuary.

But I had a revelatory vision afterwards, standing with a cup of coffee in Fellowship Hall. It may not have led me to the Lord, but it led me to this church. As I was exchanging pleasantries, a gentleman swept by immaculately attired in a suit the color of a fire engine, elegantly topped with a sporty cap of the same brazen color. He was turned out with the precision and care of a British colonel on parade.

He seemed to be on a mission of some sort.

He was carrying a mop!

He was the sexton!

And this is how he joyfully dressed for work!

I could see that in this, his working world, he had earned the respect and right to dress however he pleased and, moreover, was being valued for it. In an instant, I got a glimpse of the character of the church. I saw that he moved easily among the parishioners who were mostly of another race. They greeted him as an equal. He would stop and chat. And there seemed to be no hierarchy, no accommodating laughter or forced camaraderie. He was just a guy dressed – *really nicely dressed* – in outrageous red, holding a mop, mixing with others who happened to be Presbyterians.

In this visually dissonant but strangely harmonious tableau, I found my church. These people apparently looked to the inside. No lifted eyebrows. No sniff of censure. Not even a conscious awareness of any difference. They knew that Lee, irrespective of earthly raiment, was an equal before the Throne.

I came to know him as a rock solid servant of God: Lee Hall, our beloved sexton of thirty-three years.

Dr. Oswald Delgado

by Mary Nusbickel

When we moved here in 1945, we understood that there was an agreement between Orlando and Winter Park that there would be no Presbyterian church in Winter Park and no Congregational church in Orlando.

We joined the Congregational church after about two years. Then we heard about Oswald Delgado starting a Presbyterian Church at the Winter Park Woman's Club. We visited there once and knew that was for us!

When Dr. Delgado's reputation spread, the Winter Park Presbyterian Church grew by leaps and bounds! By the time our beautiful Sanctuary was finished, Dr. Delgado preached the people in! The Sanctuary and most of Fellowship Hall were filled every Sunday.

When Dr. Delgado visited the Sunday School classes (mine were the 4- and 5-year-olds), he was so relaxed and friendly to the children. Delia and Oswald Delgado had three lovely children – David, John, and Helen. David and my son Chip were very close friends. Delia and I were in college (now FSU) together.

Can I Play Too?

by Mary Con Miller

In the 1960s we lived across the street from a family whose mother taught piano lessons. Oswald Delgado brought his daughter Helen there for lessons.

In our driveway, we had a basketball hoop where neighbor kids often gathered to play B-ball. He would get out of his car and call the kids by name – "Hi Steve, Lynn, Wally, Ken."

Oswald would then ask "Can I play too?" He knew all of the kids from youth night and Sunday School.

I observed all this from my kitchen window.

Birdman

by Bob Case

After Dr. Delgado retired, the interim minister was Dr. Calvin Reid, the Bird Man of Winter Park Presbyterian Church. He had a what-not table set up beside the podium with three shelves covered with ceramic birds. Each Sunday he would present a children's sermon based on the foibles of different birds of Wingdom. These birds' characteristics were very humanlike. The moral each week was simple but unquestionable. The kids, young *and* old, enjoyed it. Many adults thought it was the better sermon of the day.

When we moved to Oklahoma, I started giving the children's sermon at our church there, based on Dr. Reid's book, *Bird Life in Wingdom*. The high-school art teacher was in our group, and each week she would illustrate the story on a large art board. Also, at the end of the story the kids would sing "Jesus loves the little birdies, all the birdies of the world." This was sung to the tune of "Jesus Loves the Little Children."

Patches, Our Church Cat

by Jay Van Hook

One of the things that impressed me most when we joined WPPC was that the church had a cat. The cat's name was Patches and she wandered at will around the church campus. A church that has a cat can't be all bad, it seemed to me. Patches was known to walk in on committee meetings, and I recall her at least once walking down the aisle during the worship service.

I realized how unusual it is for a church to have a cat when, one Sunday, some of my relatives were visiting and read this announcement in our bulletin: "MEOW! MEOW! We are running low on cat food. Please contribute." They thought that was very funny. But Patches was part of the church family and her food needs were regularly announced in the bulletin.

She even got her veterinarian care at no cost, because Dr. McAbee recognized her as the cat that went to preschool with his daughter! He was happy to give her good care.

I shall never forget the Sunday when Larry announced Patches' death. Usually Larry's announcements of a death in the church family were received with respectful silence. But when he said that Patches had died, an audible "ahhh" was heard throughout the whole congregation.

Patches is, for some of us, an important part of the history of WPPC, and many remember her fondly.

Living Resources at WPPC

by Edmund C. Short, Ed.D.
WPPC member since 2001

(The following is an example of studies and work accomplished by retired and active members of WPPC today. These past achievements are available for this church as we honor the past and look to the future with resources that are living within our midst.)

Having been a school teacher and a teacher educator, I have primarily written books and articles for teachers and school leaders. My most successful book was *Contemporary Thought for Public School Curriculum*. It consisted of a set of readings on the nature, purposes, quality, and planning of school curriculum, grades 1 through 12. Another book, *Competence*, dealt with the meaning and acquisition of competence in educational settings. *Forms of Curriculum Inquiry* addresses seventeen different kinds of research useful in studying curriculum. *Leaders in Curriculum Studies* was a book in which eighteen professors of curriculum (retired or near retirement) shared their views on curriculum and commented on their career-long contributions to the field of Curriculum Studies.

Beyond these books, I have written a great number of journal articles on topics such as curriculum development and design; curriculum theory and research; curriculum for teacher education and the university at large; and curriculum policy, analysis, and research.

Dr. Al Wins National Award

by Max Reed

In the spring of 2009, long-time Chancel Choir member Bob Reed, while reading a Presbyterian publication, spotted the notice of a competition to recognize outstanding religious music directors.

The awarding organization was the National Religious Music Week Alliance, a nonprofit organization that exists to encourage and reward excellence among church musicians and offers scholarships to those wishing to enter the field. It is the only organization giving national recognition to ministers of music for the work they do within their congregations and in the community.

Bob passed the notice on to Choir President George Sumrall, who also recognized the possibilities, and began the application process by completing the paper work, citing our Director of Music, Dr. Al Holcomb. Bob, the author of several reference and religious humor books, agreed to write the required citation, and the application was submitted.

Some weeks later, much to the delight of Bob, George, your writer, and the entire choir, we received word that Al was one of the six national winners! We quickly made plans for honoring him on the appropriate Sunday. This is the inscription on the plaque that accompanied the award.

NATIONAL RELIGIOUS MUSIC WEEK ALLIANCE
Award of Distinction

DR. AL HOLCOMB
WINTER PARK PRESBYTERIAN CHOIR

For developing and maintaining one of our nation's finest worship music programs.

Celebrating National Religious Music Week
September 20–27, 2009

The entire process had been kept secret from Al, as were arrangements for the public awarding ceremony. So he was completely surprised when the September 20, 2009 worship service included the presentation, and a reception honoring him followed the service.

The winning citation follows.

TOMORROW ARRIVED THIS MORNING!

Dr. Al Holcomb exemplifies that simple phrase. He provides outstanding, forward-thinking, and vibrant progressive approaches to the music program at the Winter Park (Florida) Presbyterian Church (WPPC).

He has been involved with our music program for more than seven years. Under his leadership, the music programs have grown and prospered. We now enjoy the reputation of providing the best Protestant music program in the central Florida area—a hotbed of white-haired, rather conservative retirees.

Al first joined our program in this suburb of Orlando as Assistant Director of Music. As a handsome and personable Associate Professor at the University of Central Florida (UCF), the mid-forties scholar brought with him a solid background in music education, coupled with leadership skills and a caring and devout Christian belief.

He assumed the position of Director of the program upon the resignation of a rather stern but musically renowned leader, who concentrated on the small Chancel Choir. Al broadened the scope of the position, established new music groups, and created an atmosphere of "family" in the Chancel Choir. That Choir is now a close-knit fellowship community who worship, sing, lunch, and party together.

He has done this as the single Director, for the church did not replace him as Assistant Director. Having mastered the Art of Choir Chair Placement 101, Al has worked passionately with a quiet and sustained energy, resulting in occasional exhaustion.

Under his leadership, the number of participants in the Chancel Choir has grown from twenty to thirty-plus extremely dedicated persons. Some are semi- or professional – but unpaid – musicians (including high school and college music teachers) who have joined the Chancel Choir to sing under a dedicated and inspired leader who is at the top of his game. They have been rewarded with disciplined teaching moments, where even accomplished singers learn.

Al has developed an eclectic repertoire/mix of standard/classical church music with new and innovative modern numbers that challenge both the experienced and amateur songsters in the Chancel Choir. Older members of the choir (who mirror the congregation and are partial to the classic repertoire) are inspired by a choice of music that carefully and closely supports the Sunday scriptural passages and sermon themes – often in a modern, multicultural way. The congregation loves the sometimes surprising musical offerings that bring the message home in gentle songs that explore hard truths.

Al is supported by an accomplished organist and has enlisted the aid of instrumental accompanists and performers ranging from distinguished soloists to chamber orchestras featuring the best musicians from the Orlando theme park resort area and from the Orlando Philharmonic, Orlando Opera, and UCF and Rollins College students and faculty.

In addition, he has developed a concert series featuring professional performances and student recitals in the church Sanctuary and created collaborative events with other churches in the area and in other Florida cities, featuring combined non-Presbyterian choirs, singing the praises of God. These performances/worship services have had SRO attendance.

Our Director has initiated a continuing series of special events at WPPC including a remarkable new service of Lessons and Carols, the inauguration of live music to accompany the annual Living Nativity, and produced and conducted a now-yearly *Broadway Revue* as a fund-raiser for the Music Program. They have also been SRO.

Al supervises the volunteer Directors of the Cherub Choirs and the Praise Team musicians, and councils them in their musical endeavors. He also conducts the Westminster Ringers (raising its membership from ten to fifteen) and fosters the understanding of music in worship by writing hymn notes in the weekly Bulletins and articles in the monthly newsletter, creates and conducts hymn sings, attends religious music workshops to hone his skills, and participates in the life of the church by weekly meetings with the pastors and church staff. He also visits music participants and shut-ins who are not in the music program, but are in spiritual need. And he sweeps out the joint.

Most of all, our Director of Music fosters the participation of younger musicians in the church music ministry. He has raised funds for the employment of Section Leaders drawn from the young adult professional musicians in the area, and modest – but paid – scholarships for high school vocal students who participate in the Chancel Choir and Praise Teams.

For Al believes enthusiastically and firmly in the tomorrow of our Christian music endeavors and the need for new and younger leadership and participation in glorifying God through music. He embodies a strong pride in the past and sincere faith in the future. For him, in his witness and exemplary life and service to religious music at WPPC, tomorrow arrived this morning!

During his tenure at WPPC, Dr. Al built on the work of his predecessors, and he has been followed by equally talented and inspiring leaders.

In Memory of Mary Naughtin

by Linda Naughtin

Mary Naughtin became a member of Winter Park Presbyterian Church after her husband Pete passed away in 1983. Without any relatives in Central Florida, Mary found a home and family with the welcoming members of WPPC.

Mary loved entertaining. She and Pete always had a large Christmas Eve party for the many people they knew who didn't have family, or weren't able to visit family at Christmas.

The Friendship Club was a good fit for her outgoing, bubbly personality and she enjoyed the hunt for bargains to be used for table decorations.

She also was involved in some youth group activities at WPPC. Once she took a camping trip with the kids and made curtains for her car so that she could sleep in her car on the trip.

Mary also accompanied a group on a mission trip to Mexico, I believe, which she considered quite a bold adventure. Seems that someone was unable to go and she took the extra spot at the last minute.

I fondly refer to Mary as my "ex aunt-in-law." I stayed with her for a month when I first moved to Florida. I'm sure she's only one example of the many people over WPPC's sixty-year history who have found comfort and friendship here. At her son's insistence, Mary moved back to Illinois a few years ago and passed away February 19, 2011.

PERSONAL MEMORIES

One Person's Memories: 1953–2013

by Xandra Whittaker Roth

Xandra Roth is the only living WPPC member who was a charter member.

I remember.
When we first started, we met at the Winter Park Woman's Club.

My parents, Betty and Heskin Whittaker, the Fosgates, the Baggetts, the Calls, Frances Wertz, and many others, along with George Spohn who designed the Church, were among the Founding Fathers. A complete list of the Founders is contained in the Charter Roll in the History Room. It was signed November 15, 1953.

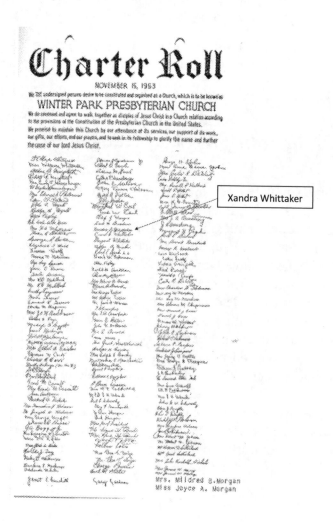

Xandra Whittaker

Initially, the Sunday School building was on the Pine Tree side and our Sanctuary was in Fellowship Hall. We met in Fellowship Hall for a long time for our church services.

There was a small group of young people – my brother David Whittaker, Nancy Call, Alice Spohn, Curtis DeWitz, and I were among the few. We young people would go to other churches for teen activities on Sunday evenings.

I recall that the Women of the Church would prepare and bring the meals for church suppers. Bobbie Jo Walker lived very near and was a regular contributor.

My sons, Fred and Dan Kittinger, were baptized in our church and attended Sunday School and 4- and 5-year-old kindergarten here. They had some great teachers, among them Mary Nusbickel at Sunday School and Mary Miller at kindergarten.

Over the years we had some fine ministers. I fondly remember Oswald Delgado. When Delia and Oswald first came to us their children were very young and so dear. My dad was on the Search Committee that called Dr. Delgado.

In 1997 my second husband, Tony, and I were married in the Chapel by Larry. Some years later, Larry officiated at Tony's memorial service, as he had at my parents' services.

WPPC has always meant so much to me – our ministers, parishioners, and staff have been a real blessing in my life.

Memories

by Alma Gordon
Retired Presbyterian Missionary to Brazil

How lovely to be asked to remember with all you dear folk the ten amazing years (2000-2010) that Alan and I spent among you, worshipping, learning, growing in community together, reaching out to the world, laughing and crying, and in all praising our great and wonderful Lord.

Weekly worship was always the highlight of our week. It came in two forms, of course, contemporary or traditional. With our involvement in the choir, the choice was made for us, but we admired the effort to meet the needs of a variety of worshippers.

Among my papers I found a bundle of Larry Cuthill's insightful sermons, probably a sample of those I really wanted to absorb in the quiet of my own home devotions. He made mention of Sir Ernest Shackleton, who in 1914 set out from England on an expedition to cross the continent of Antarctica. The explorer wrote, "There are times when our insides feel like dust and, even then, find something to carry us through." Larry, using Psalm 27 (a Psalm of fearless trust) for that day's sermon, emphasized, "Wait upon the Lord. Let your heart take courage. Yea, wait upon the Lord." An insert with that sermon includes the following paragraph. "Shackleton never planted a flag at the South Pole, he never made many of his goals, and he never earned all the money he wanted. Yet he was doing what he wanted to do, and he did it well enough to earn a place in history. His workplace was creative, productive, and enjoyable. He accomplished big things because he encouraged the full participation of every member of his team." I saw Larry's leadership of our church as an encouragement to all of us.

I also came upon the bulletin for the "Holy Week Worship Experience – 2008." It was a good example of our need to meet God in a variety of situations: stations for Meditation, Art, our Gifts, Confession, and Labyrinth. What a variety of opportunities for Worship!

In January of 2008, Larry wrote a letter to those going off active duty on the Session. For Alan he praised his "excellent job as Compassion chair, always going above and beyond."

Later we were involved in the Fellowship Committee, looking for ways to integrate folks into the fabric of ministry, and also on the Evangelism Committee. In the early days Compassion was named "Outreach." With whatever name, the committee sought to proclaim Christ at home and around the world. You know that "around the world" has always been a high priority for the Gordons.

I found an email from Jo Russell in February of 2013, sharing that WPPC continued to consider the 2013 Presbyterian Mission Yearbook as a very important book. I do hope that many of you did subscribe, whether for a volume or to the daily emails that tell its tale page by page. Brazil was highlighted, and Jo reminded the church of our continued support to Tim and Marta Carriker, our missionaries in Florianópolis, Santa Catarina, in the south of Brazil. Dr. Tim is professor of missiology and travels the country leading continuing education in other seminaries. Marta, born in Brazil and a friend of my daughters since youth, leads mission training programs. She is a capable linguist and composer of Christian music.

However, the mission outreach of WPPC is not restricted in its activities, but is beautifully multifaceted, making it a truly home church for us. The Annual Alternative Global Market has always been true to its name in that it reached into many corners of the globe, looking to include people at risk – hungry or forgotten – and doing it through beautiful projects such as those produced by the Women of Hope from Nigeria. They sent colorful hand-stitched banners, quilts, or smaller pieces that for them represented money for food, and for us beauty in our homes or as gifts. Why is the "Hope" in their name? Because they are all HIV-excluded ones with a survival ministry.

Our outreach, as a church, included Immigrants, Reforestation (as in Air Guatemala), and Mission Trips with a chance to see and do first-hand the sharing of our faith. I don't know of another church that keeps a seven-page instruction Rule Book that guides the work of each Mission Trip participant. This shows a carefully thought-out intention of doing the right things in far-away places. Alan and I had the privilege of being a part of the group to the Amazon in 2002, to Romania among the gypsies in 2005, and on Paul's Journeys with Larry's great teaching, in 2006. Since we added to these trips a visit to our linguist kids in Nigeria and in East Asia, we covered a good part of the globe, both ministering and learning. The "Accordion Doctor" brought both medical help and music to those we met along the way.

The Congregational Annual Report for 2010 lists under "Compassion Committee" many other outreach programs in which our church was involved, including VOSH, and other folk representing us in faraway fields. How proud we were of being part of a group that took the

Great Commission seriously. Even our church library, with its more than 5,000 titles, showed the vast interest in keeping the congregation abreast of the needs of the World.

Being a part of the Relationships in Action class was a continual education in opportunities of service, as very well-qualified teachers such as Dr. Frank Hellinger, Dr. Jay Van Hook, and others shared their expertise and heart with us.

By now, I would suppose that you think I got stuck on Mission? Let's go to music, another of the Gordon loves. A card in 2010 from Pat Morgan says, "I'll miss seeing you in the choir but will feel your voice and Alan's when the pews vibrate. The wood will sing for you!"

How do you like her mental image of singing pews? I was blown away by it, but accept that we loved the music program and the church, and the Lord.

Among my papers I have a sheet prepared by Bob Reed describing Al Holcomb. He titled it, "Tomorrow Arrived This Morning."

> *Dr. Al Holcomb provides outstanding, forward-thinking, and*
> *vibrant, progressive approaches to the music… . For him, in*
> *his witness and exemplary life and service to religious music*
> *at WPPC, tomorrow arrived this morning.*

That brings me to an email from Max Reed, June 11, 2013, "We all thought that Al could not be replaced as choir director, but Justin is doing a phenomenal job! And we sound GOOD! Not only are we praising God and inspiring the congregation, but we are attracting new members!" Whether she meant for the choir or the church matters not. People are seeing Jesus in a new way.

I can't leave the choir without mentioning at least one of the fun activities in which we took part. The choir presented *A Broadway Review Dinner Theater,* maybe in 2008. As I remember, the singers, casters, cooks, waiters, and diners all had a wonderful evening. At the end we were exhausted, of course, but with big smiles.

I have a copy of a note I wrote to Betty, sometime in those years. "We are privileged to be a part of the amazing music program by being in the choir." I think that this was a letter to a WPPC member asking that they continue supporting the church.

In case you think that I am through remembering happy times in your midst, I have one more important WPPC ministry that blessed my life – the Women's Program. How very special it was to gather with others in Circles or lunches or even in Retreats. I have notes on the Retreat in 2007 when I was chosen to speak on "Just a Closer Walk with Jesus." I have seven pages of it, and being a teacher who prepares for many eventualities. I will note here only some handwritten notes, highlighting where I hoped we would go in our discussions: "God gave us three concrete ways through which we can reach Him: Bible, Prayer, and Common or Public Worship."

I remember a sun-filled day, with a group of women who really wanted to mirror Christ to the *world.*

May God grant us all the blessings of walking daily with Him, whether in Florida or South Carolina, or maybe in some unexpected place where he needs our faith to shine. Thank you, WPPC, for being a home to our hearts, and for letting me remember those ten golden years. With love and gratitude, waiting to meet you in His kingdom someday.

A Memoir

by Edith Robertson (age 98)

In 1999, being the last survivor of my family and having spent three months alone recovering from a bad fall on ice in New Hampshire, I decided it was time to move to a warmer clime. At a sorority sister's advice, I came to the Mayflower. On arriving at the dining room I saw a sea of faces at many tables. I was ushered to a table with about seven others where Anna Hume made me feel right at home. She told me about the Sunday bus service and when she invited me to go to church with her, I went that very Sunday.

The following week she invited me to a Sunday afternoon performance of *Annie!* sponsored by the WPPC Friendship Club. The people on the bus were so friendly and happy that I was really impressed! Our seats were numbered and I found myself sitting beside the van driver, Alex Hines. His first question was, "Where do you go to church?" He was quite a salesman and on leaving he said, "See you in church."

During the following week, I was rushed to the hospital for an emergency operation. I was amazed to learn that Dr. Cuthill found me just as I was being wheeled into the operating room. After I recovered, I became a weekly passenger on the church van with Lee Hall as the driver. He told many stories about the church as we rode along.

It wasn't long before the Reverend David Judd invited me to join the church. Soon after that I needed advice about doctors, hospitals, and that sort of thing, and Rebecca Monfalcone, the parish nurse, came to my aid. I could not have survived without her. I hope people realize how valuable a parish nurse is to us older ones.

The church became my second family. I now have my church, my health, and my many warm and special friends and I am very grateful to all those original pioneers whom Lee told me about – especially Roseanne Conliffe who organized and worked on the parish nurse program for two years – and to all those who are now giving their time and talents to make WPPC what it is today.

Our Church Home

by Mary Jo Jeffries

My family and I have been members of WPPC for many years. David and I moved to Winter Park with our infant son, Richard, in 1962.

We had been raised and were married in the Ancient City Baptist Church in St. Augustine, so it was natural for us to join the North Park Baptist Church where we were members until our third child, Neal, was born. Richard had begun school in Winter Park and spent a lot of time with Larry Seel.

Our family began attending WPPC and made it our church home. Pat Williamson put me to work immediately. I was soon gathering supplies to stock a craft room and working in the kitchen.

We were blessed with a youth minister, Dr. Kenneth Shick, who spent a lot of time guiding our children. I remember a trip to the mountains where the young people repaired homes that were run down. They also would go river rafting where I would sometimes join them, close to Gainesville. There were also overnight sleepovers in Fellowship Hall and many other surprises.

Dave spent a three-year term on Session. I helped in putting together dinners and other events in Fellowship Hall, enjoying our members and others.

Birthday Remembered

by Mary Van Hook

The WPPC choir has always been a very warm and welcoming group of people. Even the year that we were unable to participate because of Jay's surgeries, the members of the choir always made us feel part of the group.

On the evening of my birthday that year, we received a telephone call. It was George Sumrall, and he was the contact person for the entire choir. They all sang "Happy Birthday" to me (in harmony, of course) over the phone. It was a little gesture from the choir, but it meant the world to me.

My Church-Family Memories

by John Witty

When I think back over the past twenty-six years as a member of Winter Park Pres, my heart fills with emotion because I have been blessed to walk my spiritual journey with others in the faith.

Participating in Mission trips to Peru and Cuba enlightened me in other cultures, but more important, it demonstrated to me God's love and work among people who have so little but remain so strong in their faith. Working side by side with people who didn't speak my language (and I not theirs), we were still able to communicate the love for one another and our belief in our Lord. Their delight in the little things taught me the true values in this world.

Running in the Seven-Mile-Bridge Run alongside fellow runners from my church family brought exhaustion, yet endurance to learn, train, and complete a race. Talking church happenings all along the course made me forget the pain that a long race brings.

Singing God's word in music was a highlight of my Sundays as I tried my best to not miss a note and just blend in with those other fabulous tenors. The camaraderie with fellow choristers was educational in learning new music, fun in sharing laughs, and another blessing in knowing such a kind group of folks.

Serving as Youth Leader, Deacon, Elder, Trustee, and Church Treasurer at WPPC brought me closer to my faith with each of these assignments, and I always felt blessed to serve. As a lifelong Presbyterian, it has always been my desire to serve in whatever capacity my church family asked.

Yes, I have enjoyed a wonderful walk along my faith journey, first as an active youth in my home church, First Presbyterian in Vicksburg, Mississippi; transferring my membership as a young adult to the Annapolis Naval Memorial Presbyterian Church – being married and having my two sons baptized in that church; and experiencing a full and active membership in the Winter Park Presbyterian Church. Now my journey continues as I have entered retirement and relocated to Charleston, South Carolina, and become a member of First Scots Presbyterian Church.

Yes, my faith journey has taken me among fellow believers and my life has been enriched. I have indeed been blessed! Thank you to all my church family in Winter Park. The memories will last forever. I miss you.

Blessings.

The Edwards Family Remembers

by Wade Edwards

Our three sons, Steve, Gary, and Glen, grew up in this church participating in Sunday school and the youth group. We recall Dr. Oswald Delgado playing volley ball with the youth group.

Dr. Larry Cuthill married Glen and Melissa here in 1996, and four of our six grandchildren were baptized at Winter Park Presbyterian Church.

Evan, Owen, Austin, and Melanie were shepherds in the Living Nativity from time to time. We live nearby and on quiet nights we could hear the donkey braying.

Our two oldest grandchildren now live in

Georgia. Both Abbi and Ryan attended many Christmas Eve services here and when she was quite young, Abbi once asked Dr. Cuthill what that big pizza pie window was below the cross in the Sanctuary.

Events here have included two family funerals. Reverend David Judd officiated at Harold Edwards' memorial in 2004, and the next yea, Dr. Cuthill presided at Dorothy Edwards' service.

Both Barbara and I enjoyed serving as Deacons and our son, Gary, as an Elder. He also portrayed Jesus in a Maundy Thursday service and was the Easter Bunny many times for the annual Easter Egg Hunt.

We also recall the Ash Wednesday in 2012 when Dr. Cuthill discovered he didn't have anything to mark foreheads. We went home and brought back some ground charcoal.

A Spiritual Biography

by Marna Williams

Soon after Dan Jones and I were married in 1999, we began taking trips to far-away places with strange-sounding names. We moved to Winter Park Towers soon after we returned from a trip to Thailand in early 2001. Immediately, we started looking for a neighborhood Presbyterian church. We found and joined Winter Park Presbyterian Church, and attended whenever we were in town.

In 2003, we volunteered to teach a course together at Tuesday Nights Together (TNT) based on a book by Richard Stone titled *Remembering Your Story: Creating Your Own Spiritual Autobiography*. We left town for a cruise down the Danube River from Budapest to Bucharest, planning to return home just before the teaching dates of TNT. I tucked the textbook into my suitcase, hoping to find the time between shore excursions to read and prepare from the first chapter of the book.

Early in the morning of the second day of the cruise, Dan had to go to the hospital in Mohacs, Hungary, for an emergency appendectomy. We were this side of nowhere. We spoke no Hungarian, they spoke no English. They moved people out of a ten-bed ward so we could be together.

There was one cell phone, owned by the manager of the hospital. Whenever the insurance company called to help us make arrangements to get home, the staff would bring us his cell phone so we could talk.

All of Europe was in the midst of a killer heat wave. There was no air conditioning and no screens on the windows. We could not drink the contaminated water, but they brought us hot tea in a pitcher for breakfast, which we saved to have liquid for the rest of the day. The patients were expected to furnish everything from sheets to toilet paper. Their families brought food every day. We had no nearby family, so the hospital generously shared whatever they had with us.

We got just one bowl of soup at lunch. We were able to save half of it for supper by putting a paper napkin over the top to keep the flies away. But we received a plentiful supply of the most delicious home-made bread I ever tasted. For Dan and me, it was a wilderness experience.

I had plenty of time to read every chapter of the book. I even did all the exercises at the end of each chapter. Like the heroes in the Bible who meditated in the wilderness, the book enabled me to get in touch with my true self. One of the questions in the book was "What was the best season of your life? Why?" I knew, deep in my heart, that my Golden Age was the very best for me, and I was living through those happy days at that moment, in spite of our stressful situation.

I talked to Dan about what I had learned, and we spent our precious time talking about the meaning of our lives by telling each other our spiritual stories.

Looking back, I can say that those twelve years with Dan were, indeed, the very best season of my life.

I can also say that having that TNT responsibility awaiting us at home in our church kept us balanced in the midst of our difficulties. Reading and responding to *Remembering Your Story: Creating Your Own Spiritual Autobiography* kept us focused on supporting one another in sickness and in health. Isn't that what Christian covenants are all about?

Memories

by Glenda Lowrey

Reflecting back on the blessings in life, I am especially grateful for God's plan that brought our young family to Winter Park. Hank and I felt so fortunate to be a part of the community where we lived.

This was a place where our young daughter would be educated in a respected school system and within a short distance from our home and we would have a wonderful church where we learned to serve and worship. For more than forty years Winter Park Presbyterian Church became a part of who we are (and were) as adult Christians and provided nurture to our family for a lifetime.

So many memories to recall:
• the first time we saw the light shining through the Rose window;
• the feeling that first Sunday with the newly decorated Crismon Tree;
• wonderful music and appreciation for (*and participation in*) the choir;
• fellowship and fun at many church campouts (*even in the rain*);
• youth programs under the direction of Ken Shick and Pat Williamson;
• sunrise services – *the symbolic placement of the flower in the wooden cross*;
• inspiration/leadership under various pastors that included Dr. Delgado, Reverend
   Gamble, Reverend Bass, ReverendTinkey, Dr. Cuthill, and others;
• sacrament of baptism of our daughter (*and many years later, our grandchildren*)
• opportunities to serve our church and our God.

This rhyme from our childhood comes to mind:

Here's the Church, and
Here's the Steeple
[or in our case – Bell Tower],
Open the Doors, and
See all the People.

God's true gifts: His Son, the community of believers, neighbors, and friends that support you in prayer and open their arms to welcome you back whenever you return "home." And that is the best memory of all.

Helpful People

by Gigi Erwin

As the Parish Nurse, I haven't been present at WPPC long enough to write in the normal historical sense – that is, about events that I witnessed years ago. But even in my short time here I have had meaningful experiences that one day will be "historic" from the perspective of future readers, experiences that I want them – and perhaps you – to know about.

I see generosity, love, and kindness flowing in a dozen different ways at WPPC. In the last week I've been the happy recipient of fresh oranges, picked and lovingly washed, homemade Boston baked bread, and a jar of special jam. I've seen wagonloads of toys given to the

Apopka farm workers' kids, and mounds of white socks donated to homeless men. Meals are prepared and lovingly served to homeless families housed at our manse. Then there are the many food items given to our food pantry so that a person less fortunate can have food on the table.

But probably the most impressive is the way I see people give of their time to serve in one way or other here at the church and in the community. Many times when I go to visit someone in the hospital or nursing home, I will find someone else from the congregation already there! When I attend Deacons' meetings I will hear about all the cards that were sent and the flowers that were delivered, or the baby basket given to the family who just had a new baby.

Another thing I wish future generations to know about us is the fact that these people are all very happy! They enjoy being the hands and feet of God and are truly blessed by their service and acts of kindness. It really is more blessed to give than to receive.

Not long ago I fell and broke my left femur. Suddenly I was in pain and definitely not in control. In the days and weeks to follow I was helpless and there were difficult moments, like when I almost passed out every time they tried to get me out of bed, and they had to give me two pints of blood! But during this difficult period some good things happened.

Two people from the church showed up with the most beautiful orchids I had ever seen, and then took me for a wheelchair ride outside to the patio for a cheerful visit.

I received card after card telling me to get well, and that they were praying for me. Some cards were from family and friends, but the majority came from the people in this church.

One day a church member came and brought me flowers, lunch from Panera's, and then painted my toenails.

When I was still unable to walk, another member came and took me out to lunch and then shopping, tirelessly pushing me in the wheelchair wherever I wanted to go.

Many mornings I would enjoy singing gospel hymns along with television. *Exodus 15:2* says, "The Lord is my strength and my song." It was so therapeutic!

Counting your blessings always works wonders. I now have a greater appreciation for caregivers and what they go through. I also felt very thankful to be able to be at home recuperating. There's nothing quite like home.

And so in a few years my story, an eyewitness account of God's love as practiced at WPPC, will truly become history. Yes, WPPC is a special place.

Oh, Memories!

by Gayle Ernst

You reach an age when you realize that you count less on making new memories and begin to look backward, savoring with love all the old memories.

I had the privilege of being invited to share some of my WPPC memories with the congregation. Oh dear! I was worried because, being a relatively new member, I don't have a lot of memories. Then I took a very clear-eyed look back over my five or six years with this church. Really just a few.

My first visit to Winter Park Presbyterian Church stands out very clearly in my mind. After jumping around with my family to many of the "youthful" churches in the area, I decided to strike out on my own and visit WPPC. It was Christmas Eve. I swear just about every person in the church warmly welcomed me. I was shocked but in my mind, I found WPPC that night. However, I made it official a few weeks later. Best decision I had made in a long time!

Memory #1 – wonderful, warm people. There were also the sermons and the warm, welcoming leadership of Dr. Larry Cuthill. His sermons got my attention immediately. For the first time in a while, I truly listened to what the pastor was saying.

Memory #2 – the lesson of this beautiful church. The relationship of this church to Jesus Christ and to God.

Memory #3 – the angelic notes of heaven emitting from WPPC: the music program at WPPC. Extraordinary cannot begin to adequately describe the music ministry of this church, be it weekly hymns and anthems from the Chancel Choir, or special events. Music is a second language quite universally, and our music is filled with such depth and beauty that it seems palpable.

Memory #4 – WPPC's commitment to missions. Talk about outreach. It was excitement and enchantment to hear your "campfire" tales from Peru, Haiti, and Mexico. I so respect all the good that the Mission Committee has accomplished.

Memory #5 – Christian, Christ-like purpose.

Memory #6– special events. I cannot omit the humor and fellowship witnessed at the Mission Committee fundraisers, following the antics of a totally dysfunctional mock wedding party. I secretly admit that I adore humor. And there was the backstage cacophony of getting a completely believable live Nativity presented to the public to put them in the proper frame of mind to celebrate the greatest birth in the history of mankind.

If these memories seem like only a few, be assured that they are mighty. Enough to make me realize that I have definitely come to my spiritual home in WPPC. And I have definitely found my family in Christ with members of this wonderful congregation.

Thanks for such wonderful memories.

WPPC Memory

by Jerry and Jackie Clement

Of all the ways to serve, one of the most challenging is as a member of the Personnel Committee, dealing with the myriad staff-related issues that come with church administration. But like all church work, it has its rewards – and for us, the best reward was meeting each other, building a solid friendship, and ultimately falling in love and getting married.

Our committee meetings always ran late and were often exhausting. As we walked across the dark parking lot to our cars, one of us would look at the other and say, "I could use a drink. How about you?"

Eventually that post-meeting social ritual expanded. In August 2000, we were married in the Chapel. Our plans for a small, family-only ceremony were slightly sabotaged by the CoRUNthians, WPPC's running group, who decorated our car and were outside the church blowing bubbles of celebration when we came out.

After our terms on the Personnel Committee ended, we served on Church Life. Sometimes it was truly a miracle how all those lunches and dinners came together with hardly anyone being aware of the behind-the-scenes chaos. At one dinner, it became apparent, as people were going through the serving line, that we were going to run out of the entrée, which was meatloaf. Jackie and Lynn Lyon made an emergency run to the deli at Publix and bought twelve rotisserie-cooked chickens (all that were available). Jerry was waiting at the back door of the kitchen to unload them. We got them cut up and arranged on the serving trays with amazing speed and coordination – and no one realized the expanded menu wasn't planned.

We are blessed to have been part of WPPC's rich history. Congratulations on this special anniversary!

Memories

by Jean Carolan

WPPC has been a special part of my life for forty-five years. When we first settled in Winter Park, I felt particularly welcomed by a ladies' Bible Study and Prayer group, then led by Kathryn Fosgate. We met in her home, and the group that attended remained close for many years. Through them I became involved in both church and community activities – service as well as social, including bridge-playing groups. I went with a group from the church on a trip to the famous outdoor pageant at Oberammergau. We stayed in a small Austrian village and took bus trips from there throughout Austria, Bavaria, and Switzerland. It was a memorable experience.

I served many years as a Circle Bible Study leader, deacon, elder, and Clerk of Session. My son was married in the church. My first great-grandchild was baptized in the church at his mother's request, even though they did not live here. Apparently she was drawn by the fact that WPPC was an important part of my life and she wanted to acknowledge that.

I served as Clerk of Session during a particularly difficult time when people were leaving this church. There were many problems that needed to be addressed, but I chose to attempt to help solve them within rather than leave, and I have never been sorry.

Just as I was preparing to retire, a plea came out to help with the Christian Education of children. I had some training, having served as a public school teacher for a few years and, of course, the pleasure of guiding my own children and grandchildren.

So I am now involved as an assistant to Carolyn Boyle in the kindergarten to the second-grade age group. The children who attend are a delight in that they are attentive to the lessons, eager to participate in learning activities, and learn about God's love and His promise to be with them always.

My History Memories 1958 – 2013

by Helen Condict Ammerman

My husband, Larry Condict, and I joined this wonderful church in 1958 when it was being organized. The Sanctuary was not finished, so our church services were in

Friendship Hall, and that was where we joined with our two little daughters, Vicki and Candace, and also Larry's mother, Peg Condict, who was a Presbyterian from her childhood.

I had belonged to the Winter Park Methodist Church since my teenage years, and we were married in that church in August 1947. But my husband, being raised as a Presbyterian, did not like my church. So when this particular Winter Park Presbyterian Church was organized, I agreed to join along with him, and I have always been blessed by this great church.

Larry was a realtor and appraiser and he (along with some other members) helped our church acquire the property across the back, from Lakemont to Perth Lane, from the Atlantic Coast Line (who owned the Dinky train). The train had been sold and the train tracks that crossed the property were taken up. The land was donated to our church in, I believe, the early 1960s or earlier. He was very proud of this transaction.

Other memories of our great church were our two daughters' weddings – one in 1970 and the other in 1973.

Also, we always felt blessed by our Christmas Eve services, with the beautiful red poinsettias and candles. Our daughters still remember the Christmas Eve pageant the younger members put on for Christmas, with the live animals.

Another memory, about 1958 to 1970, was our great music director, Dr. Walter Hewett, who directed our music and choir from a large mirror over the organ, on the west side of the chancel. The choir was seated on the east side.

There was a long, beautiful, red velvet curtain over the center of the chancel, but that was later removed to reveal the beautiful windows and the gold cross, higher in the back of the chancel.

Then there were two great church trips. A large group from our church went to the Oberammergau Passion Play in Germany, I think in 1983. And we took another trip to China in 1986 or '87 – that was so inspiring because the Communists were letting Christianity be accepted again, and one Christian church in Singapore had opened and invited us to visit them, which we did. The minister did not speak English, but through an interpreter, he asked us to sing a song as he played for us – "What a Friend We Have in Jesus"!

I have had two wonderful husbands from this church, Larry Condict and Clyde Ammerman. And oh so many great Christian friends and ministers – young and old – but especially Dr. Oswald Delgado, who taught me what it meant to be a Christian!

Happy Memories

by Marguerite LaRue Glennon

I have many happy memories of WPPC, beginning as a young child. I remember vividly listening to Dr. Delgado preach. He was a kind man who always seemed to have a smile for the children like me.

I remember one series of sermons he preached on the Lord's Prayer. It seemed so relevant to me because that was the prayer my dad, Roger P. LaRue, MD, always prayed with me at night at my bedside.

I remember lying on the pews during church as a young girl and trying to count the wood rafters above, or counting the beautiful stained glass windows of the disciples whenever the sermon did not capture my attention.

As an adolescent I remember Sunday School classes – learning all the books of the Bible – and fun at Vacation Bible School, which involved a lot of tie-dying T-shirts back in the late '70s.

Of course, I'll never forget the Wednesday night suppers when Bud was in charge of the kitchen. I'll never have a biscuit as good as the ones Bud gave me on those nights. He'd often slip extras to us kids because they were just *so* good!

Later, I remember spending some of the best, most peaceful minutes of my wedding day inside the Sanctuary, as I waited for my soon-to-be husband to take photographs before our ceremony. There was something so quiet and nice about being in the Sanctuary alone before one of the biggest steps I would take as an adult woman. Also walking down the aisle at WPPC with my Dad and seeing all my friends and family gathered to witness my wedding ceremony is a memory I will never forget. It was glorious!

Thank you to all the people who have volunteered over the years at WPPC – the families, the ministers, and the staff – who have made this church a blessing to the community for many years. I am proud of my association with WPPC.

Sundquist/Goodson Memories

by Rachel Goodson

In 1981 Victor, Edna, Tom, and Rachel Sundquist moved to Orlando from Birmingham, Michigan. Vic and Edna soon began the hunt for a church. Although they moved to Orlando, they chose Winter Park Presbyterian for their new church home. Vic reasoned that they weren't always asking for money! Vic and Edna soon joined committees and Sunday School classes (including the Bethel Bible series), served at the Coalition, and planned Church Life activities.

I was married here in 1984 and Tom in 1985. Two other siblings eventually moved to the area, John and Paul. John was married here as well, and even had bagpipes! Paul and his wife Alice jumped right into the choir and Alice became a Deacon and a member of numerous committees.

Four grandchildren were baptized here, Tom Jr., Michael and John (cousins in a double ceremony), and Sharon. Michael and Sharon are children of this church, attending Sunday school, youth groups, choir, confirmation classes, retreats, and mission trips. Many adults of the congregation will recall driving "all the way over" to Orlando to pick them up from school to attend after-school programs as well.

Their choir experience and musical plays led both of them into very active musical educations. Michael played the trumpet and earned a double major and graduate degree from the University of Florida, and Sharon had a life-long love of singing. Jodi Tassos, Dana Irwin, Trey Jacobs, Al Holcomb, and Elaine Goldschmidt were all huge influences to both of them. Their high school graduation Sundays were big celebrations in the family (and their boards are still behind a desk in our house)!

I joined circles, Bible studies, committees (Church Life and Personnel), and the choir. I even ran the Living Nativity one year, which is a wonderful experience, and I have continued to volunteer each year when I can. I was asked to become an Elder, and was Clerk of Session during my second year. During that time, Vic died on December 31, 2007 at age 86, and two weeks later my brother Paul passed away at age 53. Many people still recall Michael playing taps on his trumpet at his grandfather's funeral, and people still marvel about Sharon taking her ACT on a Saturday morning and then singing a solo at her Uncle Paul's funeral that afternoon. Our family would never have survived this double blow without the love and support of our church family. From cards to phone calls to dinners and receptions, they were there in every capacity to support and grieve with us.

I cosponsored a new small group during TNT, Sisters, where I bonded with wonderful women who have now become Sisters for life and my BFFs – Ann Marshall, Debbie Workman, and Melissa Storey to name just a few. We continue to meet socially outside of church and always support each other in church endeavors. I never would have found such a great circle of friends if I didn't attend this church.

Church relationships ebb and flow through a person's life, but I can't imagine not having this wonderful close family in mine!

Congratulations on sixty years, and may we continue for sixty more!

WPPC Remembered

by Jean Cumming

The Norman Cumming family became a part of this church in 1960, when Dr. Delgado was the minister and there were red velvet drapes behind the Communion Table and the choir members faced each other!

We became involved in the life of the church right away. Jean sang in the choir and helped with Sunday School and VBS (but not as much as some members do today!).

Our daughter, Tracey, was married by Dr. Bruce Cumming (an associate minister and no relation). She too sang in the youth group. The director was always called Sir. He was not known by any other name!

Pastor Ken Borden was the youth director then. And most of all, there was learning about the love of Jesus, which was felt in the church.

Our son Brian and other daughter Nancy were baptized here as well. Brian remembers the Boy Scout program and the fun he had being a part of the group. He thanks the church for supporting such a good organization. He too sang in the choir, but when his voice changed, he dropped out "for the good of the congregation."

Nancy remembers the playground with concrete culverts to crawl through and the big pine trees. She got her first kitten there from a litter brought by a fellow church member. Was it Rachel LaRue?

To look at the physical plant, not much has changed, and when you think of the spiritual life of the church – why that is still alive and well, too!

A Celebration of Fifty-Six Years at WPPC

by Del and Marilyn Kieffner

We moved to Winter Park in 1957. Our new neighbors, Robert and Mary Miller, introduced us to WPPC and we joined. The four of us, best friends ever since, are still there. Back in 1957 we had daughters Lynn, 2½, and Kay, 6 months. The Millers had a son, Steve, same age as Lynn. Robert ran Miller Hardware – and his son Steve runs it now. Del was the band instructor at Edgewater High School. In 1957 WPPC was only four years old, but it was a large, active, and growing church under the leadership of Dr. Oswald Delgado.

Services were held in Fellowship Hall in 1957, as the Sanctuary wasn't built until 1959. The Delgados lived in the manse, part of the original construction. Interestingly, a small-gauge rail line known as the Dinky Railroad ran behind the church where there is now a drainage ditch. It connected points east of Winter Park with the Rollins campus at Genius Drive and possibly points further west.

In time, our daughters attended WPPC's kindergarten. After kindergarten, they were active in many WPPC programs all the way through high school, including Sunday School, youth choir, and a very active youth program under Ken Borden (the kids called him Padre). We remember being active in a really popular Sunday School class led by Theresa Scott. At its peak, it filled up half of Fellowship Hall. We were sorry to see it end. We didn't take sides in the conflict of the early 1980s. Even though we saw some others leave WPPC then or even later, we felt a deep connection and stayed. It was our church! We both usher at this time.

We remember Dr. Oswald Delgado as a wonderful pastor. He conducted services with dignity, intellect, and respect for the Sanctuary as God's house. He spoke distinctly and deliberately at an easy-to-follow pace. People listened. During his sermons and prayers, other than for his voice, you could hear a pin drop.

On Easter, Thanksgiving, and Christmas we had to arrive a half hour early to get a seat in the Sanctuary. Our favorite Delgado sermon was titled "Come Before Winter," based on Paul's Second Epistle to Timothy, entreating him to have courage and come to Rome. Dr. Delgado delivered this sermon annually to the congregation, I think in the Advent season, and we all loved it. He later included the text of this sermon in a book of his favorite sermons, which we acquired, appropriately titled *Come Before Winter*.

Remembrances

by Drs. Marianna and Roger LaRue

When I think of our church, WPPC, I think of our beautiful Sanctuary, the good folks of the congregation, activities, and the ministers we have had since I joined on Palm Sunday in 1963. I especially think of dear Dr. Delgado. He was spiritual, firm, and serious, rather formal, yet a very kindhearted leader of the church. He was quiet and unassuming in demeanor and always wore clerical robes at the altar and pulpit.

Our Sanctuary was strictly used only for worship and sacraments. Any plays or slightly secular musicals were in Fellowship Hall. I recall he once told me that he carefully avoided any knowledge of what any of our members contributed financially – he didn't want to know. His sermons were Bible-based, thought-provoking, serious, and often quite humorous as well. He particularly preached one – "Come Before Winter" – each Advent season.

While he was minister our Sunday School and VBS were vibrant under the Director of Religious Education, Pat Williamson. It was fun to go to these activities and they were Bible filled as well.

The Sunday congregation many times overflowed into Fellowship Hall. We had lively Bible studies. And I remember some of the well-attended monthly Wednesday night church dinners at Sid and Sarah Ward's home.

We also had many service projects, including our Living Nativity, which continues yearly. We also always had 10:00 a.m. Christmas Day worship services at which no collection was taken. We had Easter sunrise service and started the flower-cross tradition.

Dr. Delgado also cared for his flock in a personal way. He invited our son Patrick, then about age 10, to accompany him to a football game. It was a great gift for Patrick to be with him, one on one. We always got out of worship services Sunday in plenty of time so Dr. Delgado could get to see his NFL games!

In remembering the wonderful music we had over the years, Walter Hewitt, aka Sir, stands out. He directed the choir from the organ, which he also played. The choir loft had an arrangement of mirrors to facilitate this. Also Sir had quite large, well-disciplined children and youth choirs. Cindy Nants is a product of this. Our high school group was large and lively with Ken Borden and Ken Shick as associate minister for youth.

I remember when one of our associate pastors, Reverend Van Dyke, retired due to medical reasons, and our congregation gave him (as a surprise) a camper, and after worship we all went out to the pine-tree side of the church lot to marvel over it. We also planted a little magnolia tree in his honor. It is now quite large as it stands just east of the front of the Sanctuary choir door. When Dr. Delgado retired we gave him the house in which he had been living and that had served as our/his manse on Fawcett Road. We then changed to providing more salary benefits so the senior minister could provide for his own residence wherever he wished. That freed up our campus manse for other purposes, such as our current Family Promise project.

We had many learned and inspirational sermons over the years from Glenn Bass, Bob Gray, John Calvin Reid, and others. We can also still recall the stress and trauma of another minister from which Bob Gray and (over many years) Dr. Cuthill helped our congregation recover before he also retired.

Our daughter Marguerite married in her church home where she, Rachel, and Patrick were baptized as infants and raised with Sunday School and VBS and church worship. It was 1995 and Dr. Cuthill had been our senior pastor about a year. It was very special that he and the session allowed a local Catholic priest to participate with him in the marriage ceremony. Thus began a good feeling with the in-laws! It also might have helped that our church looks somewhat Catholic (except for the crucifix). Our Sanctuary was beautiful that evening with candles and lots of multicolored flowers. That day, I entered the church for the first time through the back kitchen door, to process down the aisle!

Now, we have memories of our visiting grandchildren going to the front of the Sanctuary for the children's lesson.

APPENDICES

Appendix A
WPPC Timeline, 1953–2013: Pastors and Staff

Year	Senior Pastors	Associate Pastors (or equivalent)	DCEs	Music Directors	Organists	Kindergarten / Preschool Directors	Church Admin.
1953	Lantz	-	-	-	-	-	-
1954	Lantz Forrer	-	-	-	-	-	-
1955	Forrer Delgado	-	Drylie	-	-	-	-
1956	Delgado	-	Drylie	-	-	-	-
1957	Delgado	-	Drylie	-	-	-	-
1958	Delgado	-	Drylie	-	-	-	-
1959	Delgado	-	Bennett	Whitacre	-	Bailey	-
1960	Delgado	-	Bennett	Whitacre	-	Miller	-
1961	Delgado	Bartges	Bennett	Whitacre Bedell	-	Miller	-
1962	Delgado	Bartges	Bennett	Bedell Hewitt	Hewitt	Miller	-
1963	Delgado	Bartges	Bennett	Hewitt	Hewitt	Miller	-
1964	Delgado	Van Dyke	Bennett	Hewitt	Hewitt	Miller	-
1965	Delgado	Van Dyke	Bennett	Hewitt	Hewitt	Miller	-
1966	Delgado	Van Dyke	Bennett	Hewitt	Hewitt	Miller	-
1967	Delgado	Van Dyke	Bennett	Hewitt	Hewitt	Miller	-
1968	Delgado	Van Dyke Borden	Bennett	Hewitt	Hewitt	Miller	-
1969	Delgado	Borden Cumming	Bennett	Hewitt	Hewitt	Miller	-
1970	Delgado	Borden Cumming McClure	-	Hewitt	Hewitt	Miller	-
1971	Delgado	Borden Cumming McClure	-	Hewitt	Hewitt	Miller	-
1972	Delgado	Borden Cumming McClure	-	Hewitt	Hewitt	Miller	-
1973	Delgado	Borden Cumming McClure	Williamson	Hewitt	Hewitt	Miller	-
1974	Delgado	Borden Cumming McClure	Williamson	Hewitt Farrow	Hewitt	Miller	-
1975	Delgado	Cumming McClure	Williamson	Farrow	-	Miller	-
1976	Delgado	Cumming Schick	Williamson	Farrow Riddle	Baker	Miller	Arentson

Year	Senior Pastors	Associate Pastors (or equivalent)	DCEs	Music Directors	Organists	Kindergarten / Preschool Directors	Church Admin.
1977	Delgado	Cumming Schick	Williamson	Riddle	Baker	Miller	Arentson
1978	Delgado	Cumming Schick Bass	Williamson	Riddle	Baker Atkisson	Miller	Arentson
1979	Delgado	Cumming Schick Bass	Williamson	Riddle	Atkisson	Miller	Arentson Sigler
1980	Delgado Reid (Int)	Cumming Schick Bass	Williamson	Riddle	Atkisson	-	Sigler
1981	Reid (Int) Anderson	Cumming Schick Bass	Williamson	Riddle	Atkisson Edwards	-	-
1982	Anderson	Cumming Schick Bass	Williamson	Riddle Irwin (Int)	Edwards	-	Puckett
1983	Anderson	Cumming Schick Bass	Williamson	Irwin (Int) Riddle Winchell	Edwards Winchell	-	Puckett
1984	Anderson	Erwin Schick Bass Cumming	Williamson	Winchell	Winchell	Park	Puckett
1985	Anderson	Erwin Spransy	Williamson	Winchell	Winchell	Park	Puckett
1986	Anderson	Erwin Spransy McLean	Williamson	Winchell Irwin	Winchell Jennings	Park	-
1987	Anderson	Erwin Spransy McLean	Williamson	Irwin	Jennings	Park	-
1988	Anderson	Erwin Spransy McLean	Williamson	Irwin	Jennings	Park	-
1989	Anderson Gray (Int)	Erwin Spransy McLean	Williamson	Irwin	Jennings Wallace	Park Bensinger	-
1990	Gray (Int)	Gamble	Williamson Baugh (Int)	Irwin	Wallace	Bensinger	-
1991	Gray (Int)	Gamble Ruff	-	Irwin	Wallace	Bensinger	-
1992	Gray (Int)	Gamble Ruff	-	Irwin	Wallace	Bensinger	-
1993	Gray (Int) Cuthill	Gamble Ruff	-	Irwin	Wallace	Bensinger	Stutler

Year	Senior Pastors	Associate Pastors (or equivalent)	DCEs	Music Directors	Organists	Kindergarten / Preschool Directors	Church Admin.
1994	Cuthill	Ruff Simmons	Salter	Irwin	Wallace	Bensinger	Stutler
1995	Cuthill	Simmons Tinkey	Salter	Irwin	Wallace	Bensinger	Stutler
1996	Cuthill	Simmons Tinkey	Salter Bensinger (Int)	Irwin	Wallace	Bensinger Alford	Stutler
1997	Cuthill	Simmons Tinkey Judd	Bensinger (Int) Sayles	Irwin	Wallace	Alford	-
1998	Cuthill	Tinkey Judd	Sayles	Irwin	Wallace	Alford Bensinger (Int)	Lovse
1999	Cuthill	Tinkey Judd	Sayles	Irwin Day	Wallace	Bensinger (Int) Zinssar	Lovse
2000	Cuthill	Tinkey Judd	Sayles	Day Jacobs	-	Zinssar	Lovse
2001	Cuthill	Tinkey Judd	Sayles	Jacobs	-	Zinssar	Lovse
2002	Cuthill	Judd	Sayles	Jacobs	Grace	Zinssar	Lovse
2003	Cuthill	Judd	Sayles	Jacobs	Grace	Zinssar	-
2004	Cuthill	Judd	Sayles	Holcomb	Grace	Zinssar	Eargle
2005	Cuthill	-	Sayles	Holcomb	Grace	Zinssar	Eargle Hoopper
2006	Cuthill	-	Sayles Brewer	Holcomb	Grace	Zinssar	Hoopper
2007	Cuthill	Branch-Trevathan	Brewer	Holcomb	Grace	Zinssar	Hoopper
2008	Cuthill	Branch-Trevathan	-	Holcomb	Grace	Zinssar	Hoopper
2009	Cuthill	Branch-Trevathan	-	Holcomb	Grace	Zinssar	Hoopper
2010	Cuthill	-	Morgan	Holcomb	Grace	Zinssar	Hoopper
2011	Cuthill	-	Morgan	Holcomb Chase	Grace Ritchie	Zinssar	Hoopper Brinsley
2012	Cuthill Rogers-Martin (Int)	-	Morgan	Chase	Ritchie Kent	Zinssar	Brinsley
2013	Rogers-Martin (Int)	Tinkey	Morgan	Chase	Kent	Zinssar	Brinsley

Appendix B
Full Names in Alphabetical Order, with Roles Referenced

Name, Notes	Role	Name, Notes	Role
ALFORD, Ms. Dee Dee	Preschool Dir.	IRWIN, Ms. Dana	Music Director
ANDERSON, Dr. Sherwood	Sr. Pastor	JACOBS, Mr. Trey	Music Director
ARENTSON, Mr. Richard E.	Church Admin.	JENNINGS, Ms. Elizabeth R.	Organist
ATKISSON, Ms. Katherine	Organist	JUDD, Rev. David F.	Assoc. Pastor
BAILEY, Ms. Virginia	Preschool Dir.	KENT, Mr. Bill	Organist
BAKER, Ms. Helen L.	Organist	LANTZ, Glenn Otto	Sr. Pastor
BARTGES, Rev. D. Clyde	Assoc. Pastor	LOVSE, Ms. Marilyn	Church Admin.
BASS, Rev. Alden Glenn	Assoc. Pastor	McCLURE, Rev. Joe S.	Assoc. Pastor
BAUGH, Mr. Tom	DCE (Int)	McLEAN, Rev. Daniel Albert	Assoc. Pastor
BEDELL, Mr. Ernest	Music Director	MILLER, Mrs. Mary L.	Preschool Dir.
BENNETT, Ms. Imogene	DCE	MORGAN, Ms. Pat	DCE
BENSINGER, Ms. Anne	Preschool Dir. (Int), DCE (Int)	PARK, Ms. Eva	Preschool Dir.
BORDEN, Rev. William Kendrick	Assoc. Pastor	PUCKETT, Mr. Ray H.	Church Admin.
BRANCH-TREVATHON Rev. Becky	Assoc. Pastor	REID, John Calvin	Sr. Pastor (Int)
BREWER, Mr. Brandon	DCE	RITCHIE, Mr. Joe	Organist
BRINSLEY, Ms. Carolyn	Church Admin.	RIDDLE, Mr. James Alvis, III	Music Director
CHASE, Mr. Justin	Music Director	ROGERS-MARTIN, Dr. Timothy	Senior Pastor (Int)
CUMMING, Dr. Bruce	Assoc. Pastor	RUFF, Rev. Alisun	Assoc. Pastor
CUTHILL, Dr. J. Lawrence	Sr. Pastor	SALTER, Ms. Paula	DCE
DAY, Mr. Randy	Music Director	SAYLES, Ms. Barbara	DCE
DELGADO, Dr. Oswald	Sr. Pastor	SCHICK, Rev. Kenneth D.	Assoc. Pastor
DRYLIE, Ms. Helen D.	DCE	SIGLER, Mr. William M., Jr.	Church Admin.
EARGLE, Ms. Donna	Church Admin.	SIMMONS, Rev. Linda Wright	Assoc. Pastor
EDWARDS, Ms. Kay	Organist	SPRANSY, Rev. George B., Jr.	Assoc. Pastor
ERWIN, Rev. Donald L.	Assoc. Pastor	STUTLER, Ms. Brenda	Church Admin.
FARROW, Mr. Stephen LeRoy	Music Director	TINKEY, Rev. James	Assoc. Pastor
FORRER, Dr. Samuel H.	Sr. Pastor (Int)	VAN DYKE, Rev. James F.	Assoc. Pastor
GAMBLE, Rev. Robert D.	Assoc. Pastor	WALLACE, Ms. Joanna	Organist
GRACE, Mr. George	Organist	WHITACRE, Mr. Arden	Music Director
GRAY, Dr. Robert W.	Sr. Pastor (Int)	WILLIAMSON, Ms. Pat	DCE
HEWITT, Mr. Walter N.	Music Director, Organist	WINCHELL, Dr. Richard / WINCHELL, Mrs. Julie	Music Dir. / Organist
HOLCOMB, Dr. Al	Music Director	ZINSSAR, Ms. Laurel	Preschool Dir.
HOOPPER, Ms. Julie	Church Admin.		

APPENDIX C
Contributors

Ammerman, Helen Condict
Anderson, Kathy
Baldwin, Meg and Rusty
Ball, Audrey
Bensinger, Anne
Beardall, Mary
Bowers Linn, Barbara
Brown, Pat
Campbell, Martha
Carolan, Jean
Case, Bob and Betty
Clement, Jackie and Jerry
Collett, Carolyn and Glenn
Cumming, Jean
Cuthill, Dr. Larry
Davis, Alan and Susan
Dodd, Corinne Jordan
Edwards, Wade
Ernst, Gayle
Erwin, Don and Sherri
Erwin, Gigi
Erwin, Myrna

Ettinger, Donna
Gantt, Wyatt
Gehrig, Carla
Gehrig, John
Goodson, Rachel
Gordon, Alma
Gow, Betty
Hines, Betty
Irwin, Dana
Irwin Glinski, Cathy
Irwin, Terry
Jeffries, Mary Jo
Kent, Bill
Kieffner, Del and Marilyn
LaRue, Marianna and Roger
LaRue Glennon, Marguerite
LaRue Freeman, Rachel
Lowrey, Glenda
Magee, Rosemary
Miller, Bob
Miller, Mary Con
Naughtin, Linda

Nusbickel, Mary
Poole, Jill
Reed, Max
Riccio, Glenn
Robertson, Edith
Roth, Xandra Whittaker
Rudolph, Sue
Seel, Ginny
Short, Ed
Simmons, Tom and Marilyn
Singleton, Sadie
Small, Richard
Sprague, Miriam
Straub, Matt
Sturm, Dick
Sumrall, Dawn
Tassos, Jodi
Van Hook, Jay
Van Hook, Mary
Vinci, Jeanne
Williams, Marna
Witty, John
Woods, Phyllis
Zinssar, Laura

The Early Church

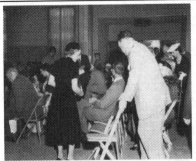

Services were held in Fellowship Hall before the Sanctuary was built.

Historical Notes

~ from the Consecration Service bulletin, October 25, 1959 ~

Under the direction of the Home Missions Committee of St. John's Presbytery, the Reverend Glenn Otto Lantz began on July 1, 1953, the preliminary calling necessary to the organization of a Presbyterian Church in Winter Park, where one had never previously existed. The Women's Club' on Interlachen Avenue was rented for Services, the first being held September 13, 1953, with an attendance of one hundred and sixty two. Church School began September 27, with an enrollment of fifty.

The Service of Organization was held November 15, 1953, with Mr. Lantz presenting a list of one hundred and eighty three charter members. Organization was under the name, The Winter Park Presbyterian Church. Mr. Lantz was called as the first pastor. Nine men were elected as Ruling Elders to form the first Session, and a like number as Deacons to form the first Diaconate. The rotary system for terms of service was adopted.

In July 1954, Mr. Lantz resigned because of ill health. The pulpit was supplied by Dr. Merle Anderson and Dr. Samuel H. Forrer until the arrival of the Reverend Oswald Delgado on October 2, 1955.

The budget for 1954 was $16,500.00, and in April of that year, the Church became completely self-sustaining. The budget for 1959 totals $73,195.00.

In February 1955, during an intensive Building Fund Campaign, $138,000.00 was raised in cash and pledges. On September 15, 1955, Ground Breaking ceremonies for the first units were held. The first Service in the new building was on June 24, 1956.

In February 1958, a second Building Fund Campaign raised $300,-000.00, and July 21, 1958, marked the beginning of the construction of the final units which we consecrate today. The first Service was held in the new Sanctuary on July 5, 1959.

Membership, which numbered one hundred and eighty three in 1953, now totals more than a thousand. The Sanctuary seats approximately eight hundred, and several hundred more can be accomodated in Fellowship Hall by opening the drapes and using the loud speaker system. The Chancel has been prepared with chambers for a pipe organ.

The Church School has grown from sixty three in 1953 to the present enrollment of seven hundred with classes meeting each Sunday, at 9:30 A.M., in the twenty-six classrooms. The recently completed section of the building also included the enlargement of kitchen facilities, additional office space, a study for the minister, and a small Chapel.

Familiar inside, unfamiliar outside.

Dr. Oswald and Delia Delgado

First Kindergarten, WPPC, 1953, Geo. H. Spohn, architect left; Geo. R. Bell, S.S. Superinten-dent; Edith Brad-shaw, Kindergarten Teacher; Becky and Billy Seville, center; Judy Jordan, extreme left

Early Church Construction

Construction of Fellowship Hall

Construction of Sanctuary

Lumber in the east Narthex breezeway

Taken from the east door of the Narthex looking to where the Sexton's office would later be built. The area was listed as an outdoor chapel and had a pulpit structure at the corner where the chair and table storage room used to end.

The covered walkway behind the Sexton's office was built first and is still visible when you walk the covered walk on the back side of the building. The picture also shows the flat concrete tiles that were used to roof the structure.

I don't know whose wheel barrow that is, but it's a doozy.

To the left of the 'Chapel' is where the Men and Women's restrooms are.

The area in the foreground shows that the Wilhite Garden has always been encircled by canopy structures. The Fellowship Hall is not shown but is to the right of this picture and was built along with these other buildings.

Curtis Koon, 2013

WPPC Construction From Above

Fellowship Hall construction ~ *early 1956*

Sanctuary construction ~ *1959*

Sanctuary construction ~ *1958*

All work completed, except CE building (completed 1965).
Photos by "Showalter Flying Service," ~ *1960*

Sanctuary ground breaking 1958

Laying of the Sanctuary cornerstone, November 1958

Winter Park
Presbyterian Church

2130 DUNDEE DRIVE   WINTER PARK, FLORIDA

Newly finished church
before Education Building construction

1953
We began with
200 members

Winter Park
Women's Club

1956
Moved to
Dundee Drive---
485 members

Drew Marshall, Ted Williams, Dennis Lawson, Jim Tinkey, late 1990s

First Unit

Dr. Oswald
and Delia
Delgado

1959
A Giant building
program-----
1027 members

Second Unit

1965
Additional educational
facilities HAD to be
provided-----
1603 members

Third Unit

Dot Carlie, Ruth Thompson, Pat Williamson,
Eliz. Brownlee, -----,1970s

Handbell Ringers in a "fun" picture at the Hari-Anna Crippled Childrens' hospital in Eustis where they played at the Christmas party put on for the patients by a group of our young people from the church. "Padre" Borden, our youth minister substituted on two bells.

1958

IT'S
YOUR
CHURCH...

Bonnie Wilhite, Sally Blake, Ginny Seel, Lillian Moncrief, 1990

Education Building
Circa 1970

Ken Shick, Wyatt Gantt, 1970s

Ray Clark, Bill Felkel, 1990

The Delgado resting place in Palm Cemetery, Winter Park, Florida

Bob Stone and Bob Shrigley
Presbyterian Women Sunday
March 8, 1998

W. Kendrick Borden
Joseph S. McClure, 1971

103

Christian Education

Pat Morgan, Director of Christian Education, 2013

Vacation Bible School, 1993

Carrie Hollman, Clown Ministry early 1990s

Vacation Bible School, 1989

Mary L. Miller Director of PreSchool 1970s

Pat Williamson Easter Sunrise , 1975

PreSchool Family Night, Jodi Tassos, Delia Delgado, 1978

1974, Parish Leaders Retreat, Chapman Lawton, Joe McClure, Robert Stone

Vacation Bible School, Chapel, June, 1990

Vacation Bible School, June 2013

Sunday School, 1986

Christian Education *continued*

Betty Gow helps
a budding artist

Linda & Charley Erd
Teacher Appreciation
Day, 1985

Youth, 1970
Now 55 years
old.

VBS students'
money for goats
June 2013

Sue Rudolph and friends

Vacation Bible School,
circa 1980

Sonshine Youth Musical, 1981

Church Life program, May, 1990

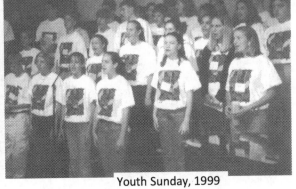

Youth Sunday, 1999

Clergy and Staff

Dr. Bruce Cumming
Jan 1969-July 1984

Dr. Delgado's family upon his retirement in 1980

Rev. Robert Gamble
1990-1993

Dr. Larry Cuthill, Rev. Jim Tinkey *2005*

Dr. Robert Gray, Ginny Seel *1990*

Dr. Al Holcomb, Music Director
George Grace, Organist *2010*

Rev. Ken Shick
1970s

Rebecca Monfalcone, Parish Nurse, and Julie Hoopper, Church Administrator, *circa 2010*

Rev. Linda Wright-Simmons *1994-1997*

Rev. Robert and Melody Barrett *2013*

Dr. Oswald Delgado, smiling, *1960s*

Rev. George and Martha Campbell, *2010*

Emily Wood
office, *1970*

John DeBoise summer intern *1970s*

Rev. Glenn Bass,
1978-1984

Dr. Sherwood Anderson, *1982*

Brenda Stutler
office, *1994*

106

Music

WPPC Youth Choirs, circa 1960

WPPC Adult Choir, circa 1960

WPPC Youth Choirs, circa 1960

Sanctuary, Delgado era

WPPC, Youth Choir including Larry Seel and Patrick LaRue, 1972

Dr. Al Holcomb receives National Religious Music Week Alliance Award of Distinction for "Developing and Maintaining One of Our Nation's Finest Worship Music Programs."

Joanna Wallace at the brand new Reuters organ, 1998

Choir Broadway Presentation Oct. 11, 2009

Bell Choir, 1990

Susan Davis, Director of Youth Choir and bells

Dana Irwin, Director of Choir, bells, and Organist

Youth Choir, 2012

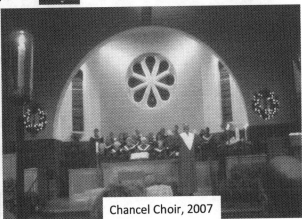

Chancel Choir, 2007

Children's Choirs *1960*

The Reuter—Walter Organ

Built and dedicated in 1998, this organ was a dream of Jim Leach (1936—2006), a WPPC member who had a great love of the organ and spearheaded the drive to make this instrument become reality.

Of its 70 speaking stops, 34 are derived from 35 ranks of pipes by Reuter Organ Company, with the remaining 36 derived from digital voices built by the Walker Technical Company. The organ's divisions are: Great, Swell, Choir, Solo and Pedal. All but the Great and parts of the Pedal are under expression. The specification allows for the playing of all types of organ literature and provides for superb leadership in congregational singing. The four families of organ stops — principals, flutes, strings, reeds — are each well represented in the specification, with twelve ranks of strings and twelve ranks of reeds, comprised of both pipe and digital stops.

Walker Technical also built the MIDI/ sequencing system and the console control system, upgraded in September 2012, which consists of sixteen memory files, in each of which are ten levels of memory, labeled "*A through J*," allowing for a nearly inexhaustible number of combinations.

The moveable console is four manuals and pedal, with drawknobs located on the side jambs, and a complete array of couplers on the center rail. There are numerous pistons and toe studs for combination settings and other controls that assist the organist in making quick changes to settings as desired.

The copper pipes in the exposed Great/Pedal divisions on either side of the chancel are an outstanding aspect of its overall beauty, as well as is the magnificent *Trompeta Real,* comprised of horizontal copper pipes located over the entrance doors to the nave.

William Kent, Organist,

Youth

80 Youth and Adults, Night of Joy, Walt Disney World, Barbara Sayles, Group Director, September 1999

Christina Mercer picks strawberries in Oviedo, 1994

Picking corn in Zellwood 1990

Zellwood Day Camp 1970s

Youth Sunday, Heather Tinkey 1999

Youth Group, Camp Geneva 1997 Barbara Sayles, Director

Youth Club, Moss Park, 7th, 8th grade 1970s

Ken Shick, Zellwood Day Camp 1972

Youth car wash, 1990

Youth Group trip to Tampa work camp, July 1997

Junior Youth Group 1995

Junior and Senior Youth Group 1990

Outreach

Romanian eyeglass mission, 2004

Carla Gehrig, Cuba mission trip, 2003

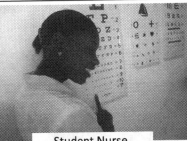

Student Nurse, Aquin, Haiti, 2012

Hurricane Katrina response D'Iberville, 2006

Flossie Hellinger, translating English to Keshua, Peru, 2008

Dr. Larry Cuthill admiring a 1953 Dodge Coronet on Cuba mission trip, 2003

Rev. Bob Gamble, Habitat for Humanity, *undated*

Rev. Tim and Maria Carricker PC(USA) long-time missionaries in Brazil

Dan and Elizabeth Turk. PC (USA) long-time missionaries in Madagascar

Guadalajara, Mexico Mission, 2013

Peru mission trip 2011

Mary Van Hook and Debbie Roberts cook for Coalition for the Homeless

Special Events

Kirkin' o' the Tartan, 2010

Cynthia Nants with haggis

African Youth Choir, January 1999

Cameron Lyon
December 1998

Lynn and Jim Youtz
Family Night, 2012

Living Nativity, 2012

Campout and Retreat, The Woodlands
Sue Rudolph, 1992

Martha Campbell
Global Market, 2011

Christmas Family Night
Supper, 1976

The Mercers at Christmas, 1992

Louise Stanley, Richard Sturm, Dick
Sturm, Myrna Irwin Presbyterian
Women Lifetime membership

The arrival of the pipe Organ, 1998

IHN gift wrap, Anne Murray,
Sandy Matrick, Marilyn Bryant,
Christmas, 2006

Living Nativity

1969

1973

2012

Presbyterian Women
mid 2000s

names listed on reverse of archival photo

Phyllis Woods
Christie Shelton
Phyllis Woods
Laura Kee
Dorothy Burk
Rita Sue Miller
Lois Ronfro
Sandy Matrick
Carla Gohrig
05-35-2004 020\ Halequine -- #31
Corinne Dodd
Martha Campbell
Anne Murry

Linda Tinkey
Babs Sayles
Helen Lucke\
Julie Rankin
Barbara Edwards
Scotty
?
Paige Mercer
Evie Williams
Roxanne Cutbill
Mary Naughton
Carolyn Holmes
Kathy Anderson
Sue Rudolph

1972

70 New Church Members
(25 under the age of 18)

Fundraising Brochure for projected new Winter Park Presbyterian church

cover

"For where your treasure is —
There will your heart be also."
Matthew 6:21

WINTER PARK
PRESBYTERIAN CHURCH
WINTER PARK, FLA.

The beautiful illustrations above are the architect's conception of what the new Winter Park Presbyterian Church will look like.

Today our congregation numbers over 250. We confidently believe that within five years this will grow to more than 1000 members and so we have started to build.

Upon the recommendation of the building committee, unanimously endorsed by the congregation, construction was started on units number A and B in October of 1955.

The location is on a plot of nearly three acres which was purchased from the City of Winter Park in 1953. The land was originally part of the old Aloma Country Club property. The new hospital is located nearby. This area is growing extremely rapidly and ours is the only church at present projected in the whole eastern portion of the city.

The manse is located on this property, and there will be plenty of room for parking, for playgrounds, and to give the church buildings a suitable setting.

We believe this is a most unusual opportunity to build a great church and we earnestly solicit your wholehearted support. It is a rare privilege to be a part of this young church with such a magnificent future so near at hand. Under the inspiring leadership of the Rev. Mr. Oswald Delgado we are on the eve of great things.

Rev. Oswald Delgado

116

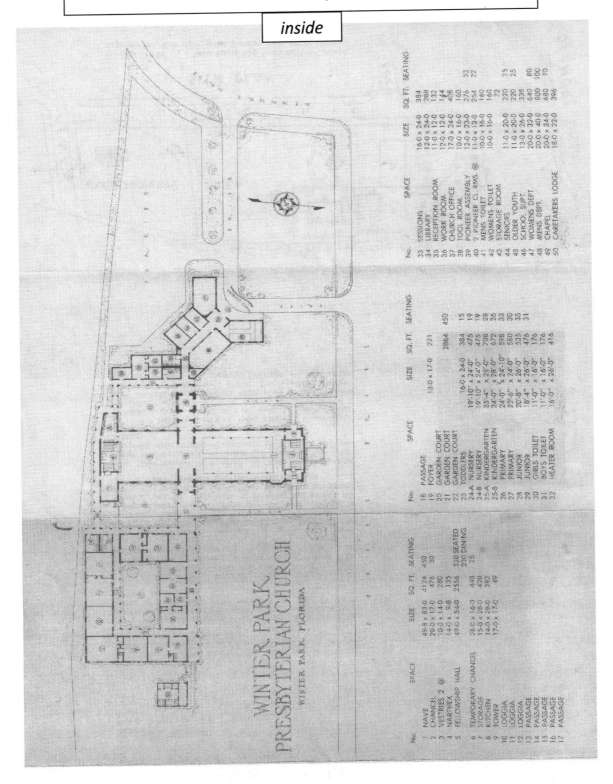

WINTER PARK PRESBYTERIAN CHURCH

WINTER PARK, FLORIDA.

No	SPACE	SIZE	SQ. FT.	SEATING
1	NAVE	49.8 x 83.0	4124	450
2	CHANCEL	28.0 x 17.0	476	30
3	VESTRIES 2 @	10.0 x 14.0	280	
4	NARTHEX	14.0 x 9.8	135	
5	FELLOWSHIP HALL	49.0 x 54.0	2556	330 SEATED / 250 DINING
6	TEMPORARY CHANCEL			25
7	STORAGE	28.0 x 16.0	448	
8	KITCHEN	15.0 x 28.0	420	
9	TOWER	14.0 x 28.0	382	
10	LOGGIA	17.0 x 17.0	49	
11	LOGGIA			
12	LOGGIA			
13	PASSAGE			
14	PASSAGE			
15	PASSAGE			
16	PASSAGE			
17	PASSAGE			

No.	SPACE	SIZE	SQ. FT.	SEATING
18	PASSAGE			
19	FOYER	13.0 x 17.0	221	
20	GARDEN COURT		2864	450
21	GARDEN COURT			
22	GARDEN COURT			
23	TODDLERS	16.0 x 24.0	384	15
24-A	NURSERY	19'-10" x 24'-0"	475	19
24-B	NURSERY	19'-10" x 24'-0"	475	19
25-A	KINDERGARTEN	25'-4" x 28'-0"	708	28
25-B	KINDERGARTEN	24'-0" x 28'-0"	672	26
26	PRIMARY	24'-0" x 24'-10"	598	33
27	PRIMARY	22'-6" x 24'-0"	560	30
28	JUNIOR	20'-8" x 26'-0"	535	35
29	JUNIOR	18'-4" x 26'-0"	476	31
30	GIRLS TOILET	11'-0" x 16'-0"	176	
31	BOYS TOILET	11'-0" x 16'-0"	176	
32	HEATER ROOM	16'-0" x 26'-0"	416	

No.	SPACE	SIZE	SQ. FT.	SEATING
33	SESSIONS	16.0 x 24.0	384	
34	LIBRARY	12.0 x 24.0	288	
35	RECEPTION ROOM	11.0 x 12.0	132	
36	WORK ROOM	12.0 x 12.0	144	
37	CHURCH OFFICE	17.0 x 24.0	408	
38	TOOL ROOM	10.0 x 16.0	160	
39	PIONEER ASSEMBLY	12.0 x 23.0	276	
40	2 PIONEER CL. RMS. @	11.0 x 12.0	264	33
41	MENS TOILET	10.0 x 18.0	160	22
42	WOMENS TOILET	10.0 x 16.0	160	
43	STORAGE ROOM		72	
44	SENIORS	11.0 x 20.0	220	25
45	OLDER YOUTH	11.0 x 20.0	220	25
46	SCHOOL SUPT.	13.0 x 26.0	338	
47	WOMENS DEPT	20.0 x 32.0	640	80
48	MENS DEPT	20.0 x 40.0	800	100
49	CHAPEL	20.0 x 34.0	680	70
50	CARETAKERS LODGE	18.0 x 22.0	396	